COMITES CATULLI

Structured Vocabulary Lists for Catullus 1–60

David D. Mulroy
University of Wisconsin–Milwaukee

UNIVERSITY
PRESS OF
AMERICA

Lanham • New York • London

University Press of America,® Inc.

4720 Boston Way
Lanham, MD 20706

3 Henrietta Street
London WC2E 8LU England

Library of Congress Cataloging-in-Publication Data

Mulroy, David D., 1943-
   Comites Catulli : Structured vocabulary lists for
Catullus 1-60.

   1. Catullus, Gaius Valerius—Language—Glossaries,
etc.   2. Latin language—Glossaries, vocabularies, etc.
I. Title.
PA6276.Z8   1986   874'.01   86-10984
ISBN 0-8191-5448-2 (alk. paper)
ISBN 0-8191-5449-0 (pbk. : alk. paper)

CONTENTS

To the College Latin Teacher

I originally prepared the material in this booklet for use by intermediate Latin students at the University of Wisconsin-Milwaukee. It consists of what I call "structured vocabulary lists" for Catullus' first 60 poems. I have divided those poems into assignments or "segments" of approximately 40 lines (usually 2 or 3 poems) each and have produced comprehensive vocabulary lists for each segment. The primary purpose of the lists is to enable students to read genuine Latin early in their training without the drudgery of constant dictionary searches.

These vocabulary lists differ from texts with running vocabularies and from interlinear translations in what seems to me to be an important way. Entries within each segment are arranged by part of speech, conjugation and declension and in the third declension by stem. Other subdivisions, e.g. diminutives, are used when there happen to be several examples within one segment. Hence "structured" vocabulary lists. The purpose of the structuring is to facilitate long-term memorization, which depends on conceptual networking, and to reinforce students' understanding of elementary morphology.

A feature of the vocabulary lists that may seem odd is that they include all the nouns, non-pronominal adjectives and verbs that occur in each segment. Even the most frequent words, PUELLA, AMO etc. are duly noted each time they occur. I have done this in part because, as we all know, there is considerable subconscious resistance to learning a new language. Pieces of information that are in some sense known perfectly well can suddenly become inaccessible. When a learning aid says, in effect, "If you don't know the meaning of PUELLA by this time, you can just go look it up," I think it only exacerbates the problem. Besides in this age of word-processing and photocopying, the economic advantages of cross-referencing have been greatly diminished. And the fact that each segment's vocabulary list is comprehensive means that teachers who use the booklet can asssign segments in any order and with any omissions they like.

Pronominal adjectives, pronouns, adverbs, prepositions, conjunctions and interjections have been excluded from the segment vocabularies. The ones that occur in Catullus 1-60 are defined and commented on in a long initial chapter entitled "General Vocabulary." Since these words belong to categories with relatively few members, the goal of presenting vocabulary in a clearly structured manner dictated presenting them all together at one time. Since it is relevant to every segment, students should frequently review the general vocabulary chapter.

v

The inflection of verbs is the most difficult aspect of Latin. Beginning and intermediate students are always tempted to guess at the grammatical features of a verbal form on the basis of its context instead of its ending. To combat this tendency, each verb entry in the segment vocabularies is followed in parentheses by the form or forms of the verb that actually occur in the poems -- except when the text form has just been given as one of the verb's principal parts. I have have found it profitable to have students translate these verb forms in class -- as printed in the segment vocabularies: out of context but juxtaposed to their principal parts and root meanings.

This booklet is designed to help teach vocabulary -- not to serve as a short dictionary. When students merely use it as a reference work in translating, they defeat its purpose. They should be encouraged to study and memorize vocabulary first and then to translate on the basis of their expanded vocabularies. When they do so, translating becomes almost enjoyable. To judge by my own experience, however, inducing students to take this approach is not easy and requires that the teacher drill and quiz them extensively on vocabulary in class before turning to translation.

The booklet is written primarily for students who are using the texts and commentaries of Quinn or Merrill. These works are cited as "Q" and "M" respectively. Quinn's orthography and readings have been used as the prototype. Forms distinctive to Merrill have been added with the notation alt for "alternative spelling." Several appendices and pieces of historical information have been added as supplements to the notes of Quinn and Merrill, which are sometimes too erudite to help intermediate students. For example, in their notes to poem 22 both editors mention the Aesopic fable about the two knapsacks to which Catullus alludes: Merrill gives bibliographical citations; Quinn adds a Latin text. In this instance, I have provided an English translation. And to add a grain of salt, as Catullus would have said, to an otherwise laborious text, I have inserted some interesting bits of biographical information about Catullus' lesser known characters, chiefly from Chester L. Neudling, A Prosopography to Catullus, (Oxford 1955).

I was enabled to undertake this work by an Undergraduate Teaching Improvement Grant from the University of Wisconsin System. I also want to acknowledge the intelligent, diligent and good-natured assistance of my sometime T.A., David Kaloustian.

David Mulroy
University of Wisconsin-Milwaukee
November 14, 1985

GENERAL VOCABULARY

Introduction

In the chapters that follow, "Segment Vocabularies," you will study the meanings of the nouns, verbs and most of the adjectives that occur in each successive reading from Catullus. In this chapter, you will study the other parts of speech, including pronominal adjectives. The nouns, adjectives and verbs of the segment vocabularies belong to classes of words with numerous members and generally have concrete meanings. The parts of speech in this chapter belong to classes of words with few members and more abstract meanings. The small number of words in each class makes it advisable to study them together.

For inflected words of which several different forms occur, grammatical paradigms are given. In them, the forms that actually occur in Catullus 1-60 are printed in upper-case characters; those that do not, in lower.

The words in this chapter are arranged in outline form, as follows:

```
    I.  Personal Pronouns (EGO, TU etc)
   II.  Pronominal Adjectives
          A.  demonstrative (HIC, ILLE, ISTE, IS)
          B.  intensive (IPSE)
          C.  distributive (ALIQUIS, IDEM etc)
  III.  Adverbs (BENE, DIU etc)
   IV.  Prepositions
          A.  genuine prepositions (AB, AD etc)
          B.  preposition-adverbs (ANTE, CONTRA etc)
          C.  APUD & SINE
    V.  Conjunctions
          A.  coordinating (ET, SED etc)
          B.  subordinating (CUM, DUM etc)
   VI.  Interjections (AH, EHEU, EN, O, VAE)
  VII.  Relatives and Interrogatives
          A.  Relative Pronoun (QUI, QUAE, QUOD)
          B.  Interrogative Pronoun (QUIS, QUID)
          C.  Interrogative Adjective (QUI, QUAE, QUOD)
          D.  Conjunctions (QUAM, QUOD etc)
          E.  Distributive Pronominal Adjectives
                (QUIDAM etc)
          F.  Indefinite Relatives (QUICUMQUE, QUISQUIS)
          G.  Relative/Interrogative Adjectives
                (QUALIS etc)
          H.  Indefinite Phrases (QUI-LUBET,
                NESCIO QUIS etc)
 VIII.  Correlatives (TAM, TANTUS etc)
   IX.  Numerical Words and Monetary Terms
```

1

I. Personal Pronouns

I/me	you (sing)	we/us	you (plural)	himself/herself
EGO	TU	nos	VOS	----
MEI	tui	nostrum	vostrum	sui
MIHI	TIBI	NOBIS	VOBIS	SIBI
ME	TE	nos	VOS	SE
ME	TE	nobis	vobis	SE

MIHI may be shortened to MI. MI, however, also represents the vocative masculine singular of MEUS, eg MI CATULLE. TUTE, an intensive form of TU, occurs once ("you yourself"); also noteworthy is the form TEN, an abbreviation of TE and -NE, the interrogative suffix, ("... you?"). The ablative TE most frequently occurs in combination with the preposition CUM: TECUM ("with you"). SESE, the emphatic form of SE, occurs in the accusative: SESE MIRATUR ("he marvels at himself").

II. Pronominal Adjectives

HIC, HAEC, HOC is a typical member of this group of words. They are basically adjectives since they can modify nouns: HUNC AD LACUM ("to this lake"). But when they are used substantively, with their noun implicit, they are difficult to distinguish from pronouns: HANC OMNES AMATIS ("you all love this [woman]/her"). Hence, "pronominal adjectives."

Pronominal adjectives can be classified by meaning as demonstrative, i.e. indicating distance relative to the speaker or some analogous characteristic (HIC, ILLE, ISTE, IS), intensive, i.e. stressing the identity of a person (IPSE), or distributive, i.e. defining a subject by range within an implicit category (ALIQUIS ["someone"], IDEM ["the same one"] etc).

The declension of these words resembles that of first-second declension adjectives, but they have dative singulars in -I or -IC and genitive singulars in -IUS.

A. Demonstratives

HIC this, this here (near the speaker).

HIC	haec	HOC	hi	hae	HAEC
huius	huius	huius	horum	HARUM	horum
HUIC	huic	huic	his	his	his
HUNC	HANC	HOC	hos	has	HAEC
HOC	HAC	HOC	HIS	his	his

Adverbial forms: HIC here; HINC from here; HUC to here.

2

ILLE that, that there (removed from the speaker).

ILLE	ILLA	ILLUD	ILLA (neuter accusative) is the
ILLIUS	ILLIUS	illius	only plural in Cat. 1-60.
ILLI	illi	illi	
ILLUM	illam	ILLUD	
ILLO	illa	ILLO	

Adverbial forms: ILLIC there; ILLINC from there; ILLUC to there.

In earlier writers, all the forms of ILLE, not just the adverbial ones, were altered by the addition of the demonstrative suffix —C(E).   These archaic forms are cited in dictionaries under the nominative ILLIC (ILLE + C).   One such form, the ablative ILLOC, occurs in Catullus 1-60: LUDERE NUMERO ILLOC ("to fool around in that meter").

ISTE ("that/that of yours") often has a pejorative or derogatory sense, which is dimly suggested by the standard translation, "that of yours." "That (ugh!)" sometimes seems more accurate. Catullus uses the word 14 times in 1-60. In eleven instances, the context makes the pejorative sense unmistakable: ISTE STUPOR ("that embodiment of stupidity"). In the remaining instances translators should probably indicate the derogatory nuance of the word.

ISTE	ISTA	ISTUD	ISTOS (masculine accusative) is the
istius	istius	istius	only plural form in Cat. 1-60.
ISTI	isti	isti	
istum	istam	istud	
ISTO	ISTA	isto	

Adverbial form: ISTIC at that place, there (ugh!).

IS this, that, i.e. a weakly defined demonstrative, equivalent to "this" used imprecisely in spoken English.

is	ea	ID	
eius	eius	eius	
ei	ei	ei	No plural forms occurs in Catullus 1-60.
EUM	EAM	ID	
eo	ea	EO	

B. The Intensive Pronominal Adjective: IPSE

Forms of IPSE are most frequently used by Catullus to stress the fact that an action is reflexive, i.e. involves the subject acting upon himself or herself: SE IPSE MIRATUR ("he himself [IPSE] admires himself [SE]").

IPSE	IPSA	ipsum
ipsius	ipsius	ipsius
IPSI	ipsi	ipsi
IPSUM	IPSAM	IPSUM
ipso	ipsa	IPSO

IPSIS (masculine, dative) is the only plural form in Cat. 1-60

C. Distributive Pronominal Adjectives

Not included in this section are distributives that are formed with the interrogative pronoun or adjective, ie ALIQUIS (someone), ALIQUI (some), QUIDAM (a certain), QUISQUAM (anyone), QUISQUE (everyone). These are discussed in section 8.

ALTER, ALTERA, ALTERUM one (out of two), another. Only the form ALTERA occurs. In poem 5, it represents the neuter accusative plural and refers to another thousand kisses. In 57, it is the feminine singular: MACULAE, URBANA ALTERA ET ILLA FORMIANA ("blotches, one urban and that [other] one of Formiae").

ALIUS, ALIA, ALIUD other. Forms are used both adjectivally: IN ALIIS ANNIS ("in other/future years") and substantively: NON ALIUD POTEST ("not anything else is possible"). The form ALIUD is once shortened to ALID: QUID EST ALID SINISTRA LIBERALITAS ("what else is 'sinister generosity'?").

AMBO, AMBAE, AMBO both. Used of natural pairs: GEMELLI AMBO ("both little twins") and MANUS AMBAS ("both hands").

CETERI other; in Catullus 1-60 only in the phrase PUTARE CETEROS HIRCOS ("to consider the other {fellows} goats"). Singular forms are generally rare.

IDEM, EADEM, IDEM same. IS, EA, ID + DEM, a suffix indicating sameness, familiar from the bibliographical IBID. (IBIDEM, "in the same place"). Only the form IDEM occurs in Catullus 1-60. It represents the masculine, nominative singular in all instances except one where it is a neuter accusative singular: IDEM OMNES FALLIMUR ("we are all deceived in respect to this same thing/in the same way"). IDEM can have the effect of "nevertheless" or "yet" in English: JUBEBAS ANIMAM TRADERE ME, IDEM NUNC RETRAHIS TE ("you bade me to hand over my heart, yet now you -- though being the same person -- withdraw yourself").

4

NULLUS, NULLA, NULLUM no one, nothing. NON + ULLUS ("anyone"). Only the masculine and feminine nominatives and masculine accusative singulars actually occur: NULLUS, NULLUM, NULLA. In 8, the nominative is used as a substitute for NON: ROGABERIS NULLA ("as being no one, you shall be sought/you shall not be sought at all").

SOLUS, SOLA, SOLUM only, alone. SOLUS is only used adjectivally in Catullus 1-60: AD SOLAM DOMINAM ("to his only mistress"), VOBIS SOLIS ("to you alone"); SOLUS...VENIAM ("may I come alone").

TOTUS, TOTA, TOTUM whole, entire, complete. TOTUS is only used adjectivally in Catullus 1-60.

totus	tota	totum
TOTIUS	TOTIUS	totius
toti	toti	toti
TOTUM	totam	totum
TOTO	TOTA	toto

TOTA (neuter accusative) is the only plural form in Catullus 1-60.

ULLUS, ULLA, ULLUM any. ULLUS is only used adjectivally: ULLIUS TRABIS ("of any plank"); ULLOS HOMINES ("any men"); ULLA VOTA ("any vows").

UNUS, UNA, UNUM one. Normally used in the numerical sense or as an equivalent to SOLUS ("only, alone"), in two instances it seems to have an intensive pronominal meaning, as we might refer to a person as "one lucky guy": UNUM ME FACEREM BEATIOREM ("so that I could make myself out to be one very fortunate person"). A masculine vocative form (UNE) occurs in 37. In 17, an irregular UNI is used for the genitive instead of UNIUS.

UNUS	UNA	UNUM
unius/UNI	unius	UNIUS
UNI	uni	uni
UNUM	UNAM	unum
UNO	UNA	UNO

Adverb: UNA together.

UTERQUE, UTRAQUE, UTRUMQUE each (of two); plural, both. Only masculine forms occur in Catullus 1-60.

UTERQUE	UTRIQUE
utriusque	utrorumque
utrique	UTRISQUE
UTRUMQUE	utrosque
utroque	utrisque

5

III. Adverbs

BENE well. BENE occurs twice with ESSE as a way of describing circumstances in general: BENE AC BEATE EST ("things are fine and dandy"). CLAM secretly; cp PALAM openly. DEIN or DEINDE then, next (DE {"down from"} + INDE {"from there, thence"}). DENIQUE finally, in the final analysis, when all is said and done. DIU for a long time. FRUSTRA in vain; cp NEQUIQUAM in vain. IBI there, then. IDENTIDEM repeatedly, constantly. INDE from there, thence; cp DEINDE. ITERUM again. JAM now; in past-time contexts, already.

MAGIS more. MODO now, just now. NEQUIQUAM in vain; cp FRUSTRA in vain. NIMIRUM surely (NEC + MIRUM {surprising}). NIMIS or NIMIUM too, excessively. NON not. NUM an untranslatable sentence adverb used to introduce rhetorical questions to which the implicit answer is negative: NUM LEANA TE PROCREAVIT? ("Did a lioness give birth to you?"). NUNC now. OPPIDO really, truly.

PALAM openly; cp CLAM secretly. PAENE almost; occurs in Catullus' famous phrase PAENE INSULA ("almost an island") whence our word "peninsula." PARUM too little. PRAESERTIM especially. PORRO further. QUIDEM indeed. QUOQUE also. QUONDAM once, once upon a time. REPENTE suddenly, at once. RURSUS back, again; in its one occurrence in Catullus 1-60 it has the nuance of "on the contrary" derived from the thought of the second appearance of a changing phenomenon: this second time in contrast to the first time.

SAEPE often. SAT or SATIS enough. SCILICET obviously; SCIRE + LICET ("one may know/be certain"). SEMEL once. SIC thus, in this way. SIMUL at the same time, together; SIMUL also occurs twice as a conjunction meaning as soon as; when it bears that meaning, the more correct form would be SIMUL ATQUE/AC. STATIM at once, immediately. TAMEN nevertheless. TUM then. TUNC then.

UNQUAM ever; always negated in Catullus 1-60: NEQUE/NON UMQUAM ("not ever/never"). UNDIQUE from all sides. USQUE constantly, without stopping; all the way to some point, continuously; once in the formulaic phrase USQUEQUAQUE ("everywhere"). USQUAM anywhere. VIX hardly, scarcely.

IV. Prepositions

A. Genuine Prepositions

Genuine prepositions are the monosyllabic words that are used with objects in the accusative or ablative cases or as verbal prefixes but not as adverbs.

AB or A from, away from, with the ablative; usually denotes spatial relationships; used twice with a passive verb to indicate the agent of the action: AB ILLO AMARI ("to be loved by that man"). AD to, towards, with the accusative; some odd uses: AD ROGUM ("at a funeral pyre"); AD MILIA TRECENTA ("up to a total of 300,000"); HOMINES AD LECTICAM ("men for the litter {litter-bearers}"); QUID AD ME ("what's it to me/what do I care?").

CUM with, with the ablative. DE from, down from; DE DIE FACERE CONVIVIA ("hold feasts starting from/in the daytime"); UNUS DE CAPILLATIS ("one out of/taken from the long-haired youths").

EX or E from, out of, with the ablative; EX EO (TEMPORE) ("starting from then/from that time"); OMNIBUS E MEIS AMICIS ("[the favorite] out of all my friends"); PUTARE EX VERSIS MEIS ("to judge from/on the basis of my verses"); EX SUA PARTE ("on his part/as far as he is concerned/as for him").

IN with the ablative, in; sometimes equals "on": IN CACUMINE ("on the peak"), sometimes "among": IN SEPULCRETIS ("among grave monuments"). IN with the accusative, into, "against" in the titles of speeches: IN ANTIUM ("[oration] against Antius"); IN DIES ET HORAS ("every day and hour").

PER through, with the accusative; IRE PER CAPUTQUE PEDESQUE ("to go head over feet/heels"); PER CONSULATUM PEJERAT ("he swears by the consulship"); PER JOCUM ATQUE VINUM ("amid joking and drinking wine"); PER QUAM NON LICET ESSE NEGLEGENTEM ("through/because of whom it is not permissible to be careless"). PRO for, on behalf of, instead of, in return for, with the ablative. SUB under, with accusative or ablative. TRANS across, with the accusative.

B. Preposition-Adverbs

Other words that are used as prepositions in Catullus and other authors may also be used adverbially, i.e. without noun objects. Such words in Catullus 1-60 are: ANTE "before", but only as an adverb in Catullus 1-60 meaning "previously"; ANTEA for ANTE EA ("before these things") also occurs once. CONTRA as a preposition with the accusative means "against"; it occurs once in Catullus 1-60 as an adverb with the derivative meaning "in return." INTER occurs once as a preposition with the accusative meaning "between"; INTEREA occurs twice meaning "among these events/meanwhile."

POST behind, after, occurs as a preposition with the accusative twice and as an adverb ("later/in the future") twice; the compounds POSTHAC and POSTMODO (also meanig "later") each occur once; distinguish the subordinating conjunction POSTQUAM ("after"). PRAETER beyond, with the accusative. PROPE near, with the accusative. SUPER above, over, with the accusative or ablative; it is only used adverbially in Catullus 1-60 in the phrase SATIS ET SUPER ("enough and more").

C. APUD (at the house of, in the presence of; with the accusative) and SINE (without; with the ablative) are anomalous; they are used neither as prefixes nor as adverbs.

V. Conjunctions

A. Coordinating Conjunctions

AN or, indistinguishable in translation from AUT but used only with questions that pose alternatives and may be introduced by UTRUM ("whether"); seen in its full form in poem 10: UTRUM ILLIUS AN MEI, QUID AD ME ("whether they are his or mine, what's it to me?").

AT but; often signals a change of subject: "but as for you ..."; occurs once as a sentence adverb in poem 30: SI TU OBLITUS ES, AT DI MEMINERUNT ("even if you have forgotten, still the gods remember)." ATQUI alternative form of AT. ATQUE/AC and. AUT or; AUT is said to introduce exclusive alternatives (this or that but not both) whereas VEL has a looser sense (this or that, it makes no difference), but Catullus' usage does not reflect this distinction.

ET and; ET ... ET = both ... and. NEQUE/NEC nor; NEC/NEQUE ... NEC/NEQUE = neither ... nor. SED but. VEL or, or if you prefer (derived from VOLO wish, will); in three of its occurences VEL is equivalent to "even" e.g. (poem 23) VEL SILICEM COMESSE POSSUNT ("they are able to eat even flint, i.e. any normal food or -- if you choose -- even flint").

The suffix -VE is also used for "or" and -QUE for "and."

B. Subordinating Conjunctions

CUM occurs 15 times with the indicative meaning "when;" it is used with the subjunctive under particular circumstances: twice meaning "when" in past tense narratives (poems 53 and 59); once meaning "since" (5); once, "although" (17); once it introduces a subordinate clause in indirect discourse and therefore takes the subjunctive (poem 4); in poem 22 it seems equivalent to SI (if): HAEC CUM LEGAS ("when {and if} you should happen to read these things").

8

DUM while, until; various uses: (21) DESINE DUM LICET ("stop while it is possible"); (44) DUM VOLO ESSE CONVIVA ("while/inasmuch as I am longing to be a dinner guest"); (44) QUASSAVIT USQUE DUM FUGI ("constantly shook {me} until I fled"; (55) DUM SIM PARTICEPS ("as long as/seeing that I am one who shares").

ENIM / NAM / NAMQUE for. NE lest; usually introduces negative purpose clauses: something is done so that something else might not happen; once with a clause of fearing and once with the negative command. NEU = VEL NE or lest. NI or NISI if not, unless. POSTQUAM after. QUASI as if. QUANDOQUIDEM since indeed. QUIN that not; occurs once with DEPRECOR ("pray against"); Catullus prays that something not happen.

SIMUL as soon as, standing for SIMUL ATQUE/AC; SIMUL also occurs as an adverb meaning at once or together . SIVE or SEU of if (SI + VEL); SIVE ... SIVE whether ... or. SI if. SICUT just as. UBI where. UNDE from where, whence.

UT with the indicative meaning as 18x; meaning where 2x; when 3x; since 2x; with the subjunctive expressing purpose ("in order that") 8x; result ("so that") 5x; introducing other noun clauses ("that") 3x. VELUT even as, just as.

VI. Interjections

A or AH ah!, an expression of pity or sorrow. EHEU alas! EN see! behold! O is used like O in English with vocatives; also like oh!, twice with accusatives of exclamation: O REM RIDICULAM ("oh what a ridiculous thing!") and once to introduce a rhetorical question: O QUID EST BEATIUS ("oh what is more fortunate?").

Personal pronouns are woven into two other interjections: ME HERCULE ("so help me, Hercules!") and VAE TE ("damn you!")

VII. Relative and Interrogative Pronouns and their Derivatives

A. Relative pronouns: who, whom, which.

QUI	QUAE	QUOD	QUI	quae	quae
cuius	cuius	cuius	QUORUM	quarum	quorum
CUI	cui	cui	QUIBUS	quibus	quibus
QUEM	QUAM	QUOD	QUOS	quas	QUAE
QUO	QUA	QUO	QUIBUS	quibus	quibus

The form QUICUM ("with whom) occurs once: it represents the archaic ablative joined with the preposition CUM.

B. The interrogative pronoun: who? whom? what?

QUIS	QUID
CUIUS	cuius
CUI	cui
QUEM	QUID
quo	quo

No plural forms in Catullus 1-60.

The emphatic interrogative pronoun, ECQUISNAM, ECQUIDNAM, occurs in the phrase ECQUIDNAM LUCELLI ("what bit of profit").

C. The interrogative adjective: which, what; e.g. QUAE VITA MANEBIT ("what life shall remain?") The forms of the interrogative adjective are identical to the forms of the relative pronoun. Only singular forms occur in Catullus 1-60.

qui	QUAE	quod
cuius	cuius	cuius
cui	cui	cui
quem	quam	quod
QUO	QUA	quo

The emphatic interrogative adjective, QUINAM, QUAENAM, QUODNAM, occurs once, the phrase QUONAM AERE ("with what bronze/by how much money?"); M. reads ECQUONAM with no difference in meaning.

In Catullus and other authors, there are frequent exceptions to the general rules for the use of interrogatives. Catullus uses QUI, QUAE, QUOD as an interrogative pronoun in 17 where a man is said not even to know who he himself is (QUI SIT) and in 42 where people ask who a particular woman is (QUAE SIT). In 40, on the other hand, he uses QUIS adjectivally in the phrase QUIS DEUS.

D. Conjunctions derived from Relatives and Interrogatives

CUR why; possibly descended from QUARE (wherefore). QUAM in comparisons, "as" or "than": TAM BENE QUAM MATER ("as well as her mother"); PLUS QUAM SE ("more than himself"); with no comparison, "how": QUAM LIBENTER ("how gladly!").

QUARE for which reason, wherefore; 5 times = "therefore" in introducing commmands; once as interrogative = "why". QUI how, why; an archaic ablative form also seen in QUICUM ("with whom"). QUID why. QUOD because; (the fact) that. QUODSI but if; literally, "as to which (thing) -- if". QUO whither, to where.

E. Distributive Pronominal Adjectives

The prefix ALI- and various suffixes are combined with interrogatives to create distributive pronominal adjectives. The forms of the interrogative pronoun (QUIS, QUID) occur when the adjective is used substantively; otherwise, those of the interrogative adjective (QUI, QUAE, QUOD) are used.

ALIQUIS, ALIQUID someone, something. These forms (ALI + the interrogative pronoun QUIS, QUID) are used substantively. Only the nominative masculine/feminine singular and the strong case (nominative/accusative) neuter singular occur: ALIQUIS, ALIQUID. The initial ALI- is dropped when these words are used immediately after or in the vicinity of a subordinating conjunction, and they usually are. Thus SI ALIQUID AGES ("if you are going to do something") becomes SI QUID AGES. The full form of the adjective only occurs in the first poem: MEAS ESSE ALIQUID NUGAS ("my trifles to be something").

ALIQUI, ALIQUAE, ALIQUOD some. These are the adjectival forms of ALIQUIS, ALIQUID (ALI + the interrogative adjective QUI, QUAE, QUOD). They only occur twice in Catullus 1-60: IN ALIQUA RE ("in some matter") and SI (ALI)QUI LECTORES ("if any readers").

QUI plus the suffix -DAM is synonymous with ALIQUI etc: some, a certain; only the phrases QUENDAM (= QUEMDAM) MUNICIPEM ("a certain townsman") and QUASDAM COGITATIONES ("certain thoughts") occur in Catullus 1-60.

QUIS, QUID plus the suffix -QUAM = any, anyone, anything: QUISQUAM ("anyone {nominative}"); QUICQUAM (= QUIDQUAM) ("anything"); QUEMQUAM ("anyone {accusative}"). QUIS, QUID plus the suffix -QUE each person, everyone: QUISQUE ("each person {nominative}"); CUIQUE ("to everyone"); QUAQUE ("in each {place}/everywhere").

F. Indefinite relative pronouns and adjectives

The indefinite relative pronoun/adjective is formed by adding -CUMQUE to the regular relative pronoun: QUODCUMQUE AGIT ("whatever he is doing"); QUAECUMQUE ("whatever {things happen}"); INSULARUM QUASCUMQUE ("of all islands whichever {the seas hold}"); NOMINE QUOCUMQUE ("by whatever name {pleases you}"). QUISQUIS, the interrogative pronoun reduplicated, has the same meaning. Only the strong case neuter singular, QUIDQUID = whatever, occurs in Catullus 1-60, usually with a dependendent genitive: QUIDQUID HABES BONI DIC ("tell me whatever you have of good/any good thing you've got"). In poem 56 it is used adverbially: QUIDQUID CATULLUM AMAS ("to whatever extent you love Catullus").

G. Relative and Interrogative Adjectives

QUALIS, QUALE what kind. QUALISCUMQUE, QUALECUMQUE whatever kind. QUANTUS, A, UM as great/much as; describing degree of difference: TANTO ... QUANTO ("by as much as"); QUANTUM adverbially: MOVETO QUANTUM VIS ("move it as much as you like"); and as a substitute for QUOT in vocative phrases: O QUANTUM EST HOMINUM ("oh -- as great as is the number of men"). QUOT as many as (are); how many. QUOTQUOT however many as (are).

H. Indefinite Phrases

LUBET ("it pleases" spelled LIBET by M) contributes to phrases like QUO LUBET ABITE ("go away wherever it pleases/you choose"); QUILUBET QUI ("anyone you like who"); QUA LUBET NOTUS ("famous in any way you wish/any way at all").

NESCIO ("I know not") is used with QUEM and QUID as one word meaning "I-know-not-whom/what, i.e. someone, something." VIS ("you desire") combines with the interrogative QUO: QUOVIS PIGNORE ("by whatever evidence you choose"); also with the conjunction QUAM ("as"); QUAMVIS SORDIDA ("sordid as you please/extremely sordid").

VIII. Correlative Words

TAM (adv) such, such a, so; IN TAM MAGNO CORPORE ("in such a great body"); with QUAM following, as ... as: TAM BENE QUAM MATER ("as well as a mother"); with a following UT clause of result, so ... that: NON TAM FUIT MALIGNE UT ("things were not so bad that ..."). TAMQUAM (conj) just as, like; TANQUAM in M. TANTUNDEM (TANTUM + IDEM) just so much, adverbial.

TANTUS, A, UM (adj) such great, of such a size; IN TANTAM CULPAM ("into such great guilt"); often TANTUM adverbially: TANTUM ABHORRET ("he changes so much"); with QUANTUM following ("as much as"); also as a substitute for TOT: TANTUM BASIORUM ("so many {of} kisses"). TOT (indeclinable numerical adj) so many. TALIS, TALE (adj) such, of such a nature.

IX. Numerical Words and Monetary Terms

NIHIL or NIL nothing; used as the subject or object of verbs: NIHIL AUDIT ("he hears nothing"); or adverbially: NIHIL MOVETUR ("she is moved in nothing/not at all"); NIHILO an ablative form occurs once: NIHILO MINOR ("less by nothing/not any less").

UNUS, A, UM (adj) one; see the entry under distributive pronominal adjectives, IIC above. DUO, DUAE, DUO (adj) two; only in the phrase DUAE SINISTRAE ("two left hands"). TRES, TRIA three; only in the ablative TRIBUS CARTIS ("in three volumes").

Other numerical adjectives are indeclinable. QUATTUOR (4), QUINQUE (5), SEX (6) and SEPTEM (7) do not occur.

OCTO eight occurs in the phrase OCTO HOMINES ("8 men"). NOVEM nine; in the phrase NOVEM FUTUTIONES ("9 sexual acts"). DECEM, ten; used in combination with MILIA ("thousands"); adv DECIES ten times. QUINDECIM fifteen; also used in combination with MILIA. CENTUM one hundred; Catullus refers to CENTUM BASIA, INSULSI and SESTERTIA ("kisses," "morons" and "thousands of sesterces" respectively).

The words for 200 and 300 are declined like first-second declension adjectives -- plural only. DUCENTI, AE, A 200: DUCENTOS SESSORES ("200 sitters/tavern patrons"); AD MILIA QUINDECIM ET DUCENTOS ("up to 215,000 sesterces"). TRECENTI, AE, A 300: TRECENTOS HENDECASYLLABOS ("300 hendecasyllabic verses"). DUCENTIES AUT TRECENTIES 200 or 300 times; used in a financial context to mean two or three million sesterces; see below.

MILLE (indeclinable adj) one thousand; plural forms, MILIA, MILIUM etc are used for more than one thousand: E AMICIS MILIBUS TRECENTIS ("out of three hundred thousand friends"); adverbial MILIES ("a thousand times").

Central to understanding Latin monetary terminology is the adjective SESTERIUS, A, UM which means "consisting of two and a half." It is derived from SEMIS ("half") and TERTIUS ("third"). Hence its etymological meaning is roughly "consisting of (two whole parts and) a half of a third." The sesterce (SESTERTIUS NUMMUS {"coin"}), the small silver coin that was the basic unit of price, was so named because it was originally worth two and a half copper asses. The word SESTERIUS was normally used substantively with NUMMUS understood and is translated "sesterce."

In describing transactions involving 2,000 sesterces or more, the neuter plural form SESTERTIA was used with other numerals to denote so many thousands (MILIA) of sesterces. In 23, a friend as been asking Catullus for a loan of CENTUM SESTERTIA. That would be "one hundred thousand sesterces."

In very large transactions, that figure itself (100,000 sesterces) is the basic unit of price. It is used in combination with numerical adverbs that indicate how many hundreds of thousands are involved. In 29, one of Caesar's henchmen is said to have wasted DUCENTIES AUT TRECENTIES ("200 or 300 times {100,000 sesterces}"), which works out to twenty or thirty million.

Given recent inflation and Catullus' penchant for exaggeration, the sesterce of the poet's time seems to have come close enough to our dollar to justify equating them. In 26, 215,000 sesterces is referred to as a burdensome mortgage; in 29, as we have just seen, a crooked politician is said to have wasted fortunes of 20 and 30 million sesterces; and in 41, a homely prostitute who wants to charge 10,000 sesterces is declared insane.

In writing, the sign HS was used to indicate that a figure referred to sesterces. The first symbol is not the letter H but two vertical lines (Roman numeral two) linked by a bar to avoid ambiguity; the second is S for SEMIS (a half). The sign survives slightly altered as our dollar sign.

NOUNS
First Declension
Feminine

CARTA scroll, page; alt CHARTA.
CURA care, concern.
DOMINA mistress.
OPERA work, action.
PATRONA patroness.
PUELLA girl.
ZONA girdle, sash.

Plural Forms with Singular or Collective Meanings

DELICIAE delight, sweetheart.
NUGAE trifles, nonsense.
TENEBRAE shadows, darkness.

Second Declension
Masculine

ANIMUS soul, spirit.
CORNELIUS Cornelius Nepos, historian and biographer from Northern Italy.
DIGITUS finger.
LIBELLUS booklet, diminutive of LIBER.
OCULUS eye.
ORCUS Orcus, god of the underworld, alias Pluto, Hades.
SERVUS slave, servant.

Neuter

AEVUM age, epoch.
DESIDERIUM desire.
FACTUM deed, action; perfect participle of FACIO.
GREMIUM bosom, lap.
MALUM apple.
SAECLUM age, generation.
SOLACIOLUM small comfort, consolation; diminutive of SOLACIUM.

Third Declension

Liquid Stems (L,R)

ARDOR, ARDORIS (m) heat, passion.
DOLOR, DOLORIS (m) sorrow.
JUPPITER (m) the form of Jupiter's name used in exclamations and as the nominative case; other cases formed on JOV-: genitive, JOVIS; dative, JOVI etc.

15

LABOR, LABORIS (m) work, labor.
MATER, MATRIS (f) mother.
PASSER, PASSERIS (m) sparrow.

Nasal Stems

CUPIDO, CUPIDINIS (m) Cupid.
HOMO, HOMINIS (m) man, person.
ITER, ITINERIS (n) road, journey.
VIRGO, VIRGINIS (f) virgin, maiden.

Palatal Stem (C,G): PUMEX, PUMICIS (mf) pumice stone.

S-Stem: VENUS, VENERIS (f) Venus, the goddess of love.

Fourth Declension

MORSUS, MORSUS (m) bite.
RISUS, RISUS (m) laugh, laughter.
SINUS, SINUS (m) lap, bosom; any curved object, eg bay.

ADJECTIVES
First-Second Declension

ARIDUS dry.
BELLUS pretty, fair.
CARUS dear.
DOCTUS learned; perfect participle of DOCEO (teach).
GRATUS pleasing.
ITALUS Italian.
LABORIOSUS laborious.
LEPIDUS charming, pleasant.
MALUS bad, evil; adv MALE.
MELLITUS honeyed, sweet.
MEUS my, mine.
NOVUS new, strange.
PRIMUS first; first part of.
SUUS his, her, its or their own.
TENEBRICOSUS dark, full of shade.
TUUS your, yours (singular).
VENUSTUS charming, lovely; comp VENUSTIOR, VENUSTIUS.

Diminutives

AUREOLUS little golden, cp AUREUS (golden).
MISELLUS poor little, cp MISER (miserable).
TURGIDULUS little swollen, cp TURGIDUS (swollen).

RUS > (E)R: VESTER, VESTRA, VESTRUM your, yours (plural).

Third Declension
I-Stems

GRAVIS, GRAVE heavy, serious.
OMNIS, OMNE all, every.
PERENNIS, PERENNE everlasting, perennial.
TRISTIS, TRISTE sad, sorrowful.

One Termination

PERNIX (PERNICIS) nimble, quick.
PLUS more; in the singular only the neuter accusative/adverbial form PLUS occurs; plural forms: PLURES, PLURA etc.

Three Termination: ACER, ACRIS, ACRE sharp.

VERBS
First Conjugation

AMO, AMARE love (AMABAT).
DEVORO, DEVORARE devour, swallow up (DEVORATIS).
DO, DARE give.
DONO, DONARE give, dedicate.
EXPLICO, EXPLICARE explain, expound.
INCITO, INCITARE arouse, incite.
JOCOR, JOCARI make a joke.
LEVO, LEVARE lighten.
LIGO, LIGARE bind, tie (LIGATAM).
NEGO, NEGARE deny (NEGANT).
PIPIO, PIPIARE chirp (PIPIABAT).
PUTO, PUTARE think.

Second Conjugation

AUDEO, AUDERE, AUSUS semi-deponent, dare (AUSUS ES).
FLEO, FLERE, FLEVI weep (FLENDO).
HABEO, HABERE, HABUI, HABITUM have (HABE).
LUBET, LUBERE, LUBUIT impersonal verb, it is pleasing; alt LIBET.
LUGEO, LUGERE, LUXI weep, mourn (LUGETE)
MANEO, MANERE, MANSI remain, stay (MANEAT).
MOVEO, MOVERE, MOVI, MOTUM move (MOVEBAT).
NITEO, NITERE, NITUI shine, glitter (NITENTI).
RUBEO, RUBERE be red (RUBENT)
SOLEO, SOLERE, SOLITUS be accustomed or wont to do (SOLET, SOLEBAS).
TENEO, TENERE, TENUI, TENTUM hold, keep.

Third Conjugation

ACQUIESCO, ACQUIESCERE, ACQUIEVI, ACQUIETUM grow quiet; alt ADQUIESCO (ACQUIESCAT).
APPETO, APPETERE, APPETIVI, APPETITUM seek after, strive for; alt ADPETO (APPETENTI).
AUFERO, AUFERRE, ABSTULI, ABLATUM carry away (ABSTULISTIS).
CREDO, CREDERE, CREDIDI, CREDITUM believe.
FERO, FERRE, TULI, LATUM carry, bear; bring words, hence report (FERUNT).
LUDO, LUDERE, LUSI, LUSUM play, mock.
NOSCO, NOSCERE, NOVI, NOTUM learn about, get to know; perfect tense = know; pluperfect = knew (NOVERAT > NORAT).
SOLVO, SOLVERE, SOLVI, SOLUTUM loosen, release (SOLUIT).

Third Conjugation IO

FACIO, FACERE, FECI, FACTUM do, make.
MORIOR, MORI, MORTUUS die (MORTUUS EST).

Fourth Conjugation

CIRCUMSILIO, CIRCUMSILIRE jump around (CIRCUMSILIENS).
EXPOLIO, EXPOLIRE polish (EXPOLITUM).

Irregular Verbs

EO, IRE, IVI go (IT).
POSSUM, POSSE, POTUI be able (POSSEM).
REDEO, REDIRE, REDIVI return.
SUM, ESSE, FUI be (EST, FUISSE, ERAT, SIT).

APPENDIX

In poem 2, lines 11-13, Catullus refers to the myth of Atalanta and a hero known as Milanion or Hippomenes. There are several ancient versions of this myth. Perhaps the best known occurs in Ovid's Metamorphoses, Book 10, lines 560-680. A more concise one comes from a Greek reference work of the Hellenistic period, The Library, by Apollodorus, Book 3, section 9:

"Atalanta was the daughter of Iasos and Clymene, the child of Minyas. Since Iasos wanted sons, he exposed Atalanta at birth, but a female bear happened along and suckled her over a long period of time until some hunters found her and raised her among themselves. When Atalanta grew up, she remained a virgin and spent her time dressed in armor, hunting in the wilderness. Two centaurs, Rhoecus and Hylaeus by name, tried to rape her, but she shot them down with arrows. She joined the heroes who hunted the Calydonian boar and in the funeral games given to honor Pelias (the king of Iolcus slain by Jason and Medea) she wrestled against Peleus (Achilles' father) and won.

18

"Later she discovered the identity of her parents. When her father urged her to marry, she went to a place that was shaped like a racecourse. There she drove a broad stake into the ground and from that point she sent her suitors running ahead of her. Then she ran after them, dressed in armor. Death on the spot was decreed for the suitors whom she caught; marriage, for the one who escaped. After many suitors had died, Milanion fell in love with her and came to the course carrying golden apples from Aphrodite. As Atalanta was chasing him, he threw the apples on the ground. She stopped to pick them up and thus lost the race, and Milanion married her. It is said that later while they were out hunting together they entered a sacred precinct of Zeus where they made love and were transformed into lions (as a punishment for their sacrilegious act)."

NOUNS
First Declension

AURA wind, breeze.
COMA hair.
INSULA island.
LESBIA Catullus' mistress.
PALMULA little hand or palm, diminutive of PALMA.
SILVA forest.

Second Declension
Masculine

CYTORUS Mt. Cytorus, a mountain on the coast of the Black Sea
near Amastris.
DEUS god.
ERUS master.
GEMELLUS little twin, diminutive of GEMINUS.
HADRIATICUS the Adriatic sea.
PHASELUS a small boat, yacht; alt PHASELLUS.
SIBILUS whistling, hissing.

Feminine: RHODUS Rhodes, the island in the eastern Mediterranean.

Neuter

BASIUM kiss.
FRETUM strait, channel.
JUGUM yoke; from the similarity of shapes, a ridge between
mountain peaks, then mountains in general.
LINTEUM linen, cloth.
VOTUM vow; perfect participle of VOVEO.

Third Declension
Dental Stems (D,T)

AMASTRIS, AMASTRIDIS (f) Amastris, a city on the coast of the
Black Sea, near Mt. Cytorus.
CYCLADES, CYCLADUM (f) plural only, the Cyclades, a group of
islands in the Aegean.
HOSPES, HOSPITIS (m) guest, host, friend.
PES, PEDIS (m) foot; in poem #4 it designates the bottom corner
of a sail.
PROPONTIS, PROPONTIDIS (f) Propontis or Sea of Marmora, the
bloated channel between the Aegean and the Black Sea; Greek
accusative PROPONTIDA.
QUIES, QUIETIS (f) rest, quiet.

Liquid Stems (L,R)

AEQUOR, AEQUORIS (n) the flat surface of the sea; the sea.
CASTOR, CASTORIS (m) Castor, a god, the brother of Pollux.
JUPPITER Jupiter; in poem #4, the personification of the sky;
other cases formed with the stem JOV-: JOVIS etc.
RUMOR, RUMORIS (m) report, rumor, gossip.
SOL, SOLIS (m) sun.

Palatal Stems (C,G)

LUX, LUCIS (f) light.
NOX, NOCTIS (f) night.

Nasal Stems

CACUMEN, CACUMINIS (n) peak, summit.
ORIGO, ORIGINIS (f) origin, source.

I-Stems

MARE, MARIS (n) sea.
NAVIS, NAVIS (f) ship.
SENEX, SENIS (m) an old man.

S-Stems

AS, ASSIS (m) an as, a small copper coin, a penny.
LITUS, LITORIS (n) shore, coast.
OPUS, OPERIS (n) work, labor; OPUS EST with the ablative = there
is need of (work for) something.

Labial Stem (B,P): TRABS, TRABIS (f) beam, plank.

Fourth Declension

IMPETUS, IMPETUS (m) attack, impetus, force.
LACUS, LACUS (m) lake.
SINUS, SINUS (m) lap, bosom; any curved object, eg bay, gulf.

ADJECTIVES
First-Second Declension

COGNITUS familiar; superlative COGNITISSIMUS; the perfect
participle of COGNOSCO.
COMATUS hairy.
CYTORIUS Cytorian, of or related to Mt. Cytorus.
HORRIDUS rough, wild, savage.
LAEVUS left, on the left hand.
LIMPIDUS clear, limpid.
MALUS bad, evil.
MEUS my, mine.

21

MULTUS much, many.
NOVUS new, strange; superlative NOVISSIMUS latest, most recent.
PERPETUUS perpetual, everlasting.
PONTICUS Pontic, of or related to Pontus, the Black Sea.
RECONDITUS secret, hidden; perfect participle of RECONDO.
SECUNDUS second; favorable -- from the idea of "seconding" an effort.
SEVERUS severe, stern; comp SEVERIOR, SEVERIUS.
THRACIUS Thracian; Thrace was the barbarian land north of Greece.
TUUS your, yours (singular).
ULTIMUS farthest, most remote.

RUS > (E)R

BUXIFER, BUXIFERA, BUXIFERUM bearing or producing box trees.
DEXTER, DEXTERA, DEXTERUM right, on the right hand.

Third Declension
I-Stems

BREVIS, BREVE brief, short.
LITORALIS, LITORALE of or on the shore, cp LITUS (shore).
NOBILIS, NOBILE noble, eminent.
OMNIS, OMNE all, every.

One Termination

IMPOTENS (IMPOTENTIS) uncontrollable, raging; "powerless" only in the sense of being unable to exercise restraint.
MINAX (MINACIS) threatening.
TRUX (TRUCIS) rough, savage.

Irregular comparative: PRIOR, PRIUS prior, previous; adv PRIUS.

Three termination: CELER, CELERIS, CELERE swift, quick; superlative, CELERRIMUS speediest.

VERBS
First Conjugation

AESTIMO, AESTIMARE estimate the value of something, esteem (AESTIMEMUS).
AMO, AMARE love (AMEMUS).
CONTURBO, CONTURBARE disturb, throw into disorder, confuse (CONTURBABIMUS).
DEDICO, DEDICARE dedicate (DEDICAT).
DO, DARE, DEDI, DATUM give (DA).
NATO, NATARE swim (NATANTIS).
NEGO, NEGARE deny (NEGAT).
STO, STARE, STETI stand (STETISSE).
VOCO, VOCARE call (VOCARET).

22

VOLO, VOLARE fly.

Second Conjugation

INVIDEO, INVIDERE, INVIDI, INVISUM envy, resent -- from the idea of looking at someone intensely.
SENEO, SENERE to be or grow old (SENET).
VIDEO, VIDERE, VIDI, VISUM see (VIDETIS).
VOVEO, VOVERE, VOVI, VOTUM vow, promise something to the gods in exchange for a specific favor; VOTUM as a noun, a vow.

Third Conjugation

COGNOSCO, COGNOSCERE, COGNOVI, COGNITUM get to know; perfect tense, to know; COGNITUS as an adjective, known, familiar; superlative COGNITISSIMUS very familiar.
EDO, EDERE, EDIDI, EDITUM put forth, give out, emit (EDIDIT).
DICO, DICERE, DIXI, DICTUM say (DICIT).
FERO, FERRE, TULI, LATUM bear, carry (TULISSE).
IMBUO, IMBUERE, IMBUI, IMBUTUM to make wet, moisten (IMBUISSE).
INCIDO, INCIDERE, INCIDI fall in or upon (INCIDISSET).
LOQUOR, LOQUI, LOCUTUS say, speak, tell (LOQUENTE).
OCCIDO, OCCIDERE, OCCIDI fall, fall down; (of the sun) set (OCCIDIT).
RECONDO, RECONDERE, RECONDIDI, RECONDITUM put away, store or hide; RECONDITUS as an adjective, secret, concealed (RECONDITA).
VIVO, VIVERE, VIXI, VICTUM live (VIVAMUS).

Third Conjugation IO: FACIO, FACERE, FECI, FACTUM do make (ESSE FACTA, FECERIMUS).

Fourth Conjugation

DORMIO, DORMIRE, DORMIVI sleep (DORMIENDA).
SCIO, SCIRE, SCIVI, SCITUM know (SCIAMUS, SCIAT).
VENIO, VENIRE, VENI come (VENIRET).

Irregular Verbs

AIO say, assert (AIT).
NEQUEO, NEQUIRE, NEQUII to be unable (NEQUISSE).
POSSUM, POSSE, POTUI be able (POSSUNT, POSSIT).
PRAETEREO, PRAETERIRE, PRAETERII, PRAETERITUM go by, pass.
REDEO, REDIRE, REDII return.
SUM, ESSE, FUI be (FUISSE, FORET, FUIT, FUERUNT > FUERE, EST).

SEGMENT 3   (Poems 6-8)

NOUNS
First Declension

HARENA sand.
CLODIA Catullus' mistress.
LINGUA tongue.
PUELLA girl.
VITA life.

Plural Forms with Singular or Collective Meanings

CYRENAE Cyrene, a city in N Africa, near modern Benghazi, Libya.
DELICIAE delight, sweetheart.
INEPTIAE foolishness, stupidity.

Second Declension
Masculine

LECTUS bed, couch.
NUMERUS number.
PULVINUS cushion, seat.

Persons

BATTUS the cognomen or nickname (probably meaning "Stutterer") of
a certain Aristoteles, a 7th century Spartan who founded the city
of Cyrene.
CATULLUS the author.
FLAVIUS Catullus' friend, otherwise unknown.

Neuter

BASIUM kiss.
CAELUM sky.
LABELLUM little lip; diminutive of LABIUM.
OLIVUM olive oil.
ORACLUM oracle, temple where divinely inspired advice is
obtained.
SCORTUM prostitute.
SEPULCRUM sepulchre, tomb, grave.
SERTUM garland; perfect participle of SERO (weave).
STUPRUM immoral action, sin.

Third Declension

Nasal Stems

ARGUTATIO, ARGUTATIONIS (f) proof, evidence.
BASIATIO, BASIATIONIS (f) kiss.

24

HOMO, HOMINIS (m) man, person.
INAMBULATIO, INAMBULATIONIS (f) walking around, pacing.

S-Stems

LATUS, LATERIS (n) side.
SIDUS, SIDERIS (n) star.

Dental Stems (D,T)

MENS, MENTIS (f) mind.
NOX, NOCTIS (f) night.

Liquid Stems (L,R)

AMOR, AMORIS (m) love.
IUPPITER (m) Jupiter, nominative; other cases formed with JOV-: genitive JOVIS, dative JOVI etc.
SOL, SOLIS (m) sun.

I-Stem: CUBILE, CUBILIS (n) bed.

Fourth Declension: VERSUS, VERSUS (m) verse, line of poetry.

ADJECTIVES
First-Second Declension

AESTUOSUS hot, boiling; full of AESTUS (heat, agitation).
BELLUS pretty, fair.
BONUS good.
CANDIDUS bright.
CURIOSUS curious, concerned, officious; full of CURA (care).
ECFUTUTUS adjective based on the perfect participle of FUTUO, a vulgar word for sexual intercourse; sexually exhausted, debauched.
FEBRICULOSUS feverish; full of FEBRICULAE (little fevers).
FURTIVUS secret, stolen; cp FUR (thief).
ILLEPIDUS not charming, rude, boorish; alt INLEPIDUS.
INVITUS unwilling.
JOCOSUS funny, enjoyable; full of JOCI (jokes).
LEPIDUS charming, elegant.
LIBYSSUS Libyan.
MAGNUS great.
MALUS bad, evil.
MULTUS much, many.
PERAEQUUS quite equal; intensive form of AEQUUS; adv PERAEQUE.
SCELESTUS immoral, depraved; characterized by SCELUS (crime).
SYRIUS Syrian.
TUUS your, yours.
TREMULUS shaky, tremulous.
VERUS true; adv VERE or VERUM.

25

VESANUS mad, insane.
VIDUUS bereaved, alone.

RUS > (E)R

LASARPICIFER, LASARPICIFERA, LASARPICIFERUM bearing or producing asafoetida, a plant with medicinal properties; alt LASERPICIFER.
MISER, MISERA, MISERUM sad, miserable.
SACER, SACRA, SACRUM sacred, holy.

Third Declension Adjectives

One Termination

FRAGRANS (FRAGRANTIS) fragrant.
IMPOTENS (IMPOTENTIS) uncontrollable, raging; "powerless" only in the sense of being unable to exercise restraint.
INELEGANS (INELEGANTIS) inelegant, tasteless.
VETUS (VETERIS) old.

VERBS

First Conjugation

AMO, AMARE love (AMATA, AMABIS, AMABITUR).
BASIO, BASIARE kiss (BASIABIS).
CLAMO, CLAMARE shout, cry out (CLAMAT).
DESTINO, DESTINARE decide, determine; perfect participle DESTINATUS as adjective, determined.
FASCINO, FASCINARE bewitch, curse.
OBDURO, OBDURARE be strong, hard (OBDURA, OBDURAT).
OBSTINO, OBSTINARE persist, be resolute; perfect participle as an adjective: OBSTINATUS resolute, persistent (OBSTINATA).
PERNUMERO, PERNUMERARE count, enumerate.
ROGO, ROGARE ask, ask for something (ROGABIT, ROGABERIS).
SECTOR, SECTARI, SECTATUS follow; frequentative of SEQUOR (SECTARE).
VENTITO, VENTITARE frequentative of VENIO, come often, visit regularly (VENTITABAS).
VOCO, VOCARE call.

Second Conjugation

DOLEO, DOLERE, DOLUI suffer, feel sorry, grieve (DOLEBIS).
FATEOR, FATERI, FASSUS confess, admit.
FULGEO, FULGERE, FULSI shine (FULSERUNT > FULSERE).
HABEO, HABERE, HABUI, HABITUM have (HABES).
JACEO, JACERE, JACUI lie, recline (JACET).
MANEO, MANERE, MANSI remain, stay (MANET).

MORDEO, MORDERE, MOMORDI, MORSUM bite (MORDEBIS).

PUDET, PUDERE cause shame, impersonal verb; it causes shame to do something = PUDET FACERE ALIQUID.

TACEO, TACERE, TACUI, TACITUM be silent or make silent, silence; TACITUS as an adjective = silent or unmentioned (TACITUM, TACET).

VALEO, VALERE, VALUI be well or strong; as a substitute for POSSUM with a complementary infinitive: be strong enough or able to do something (VALET).

VIDEO, VIDERE, VIDI, VISUM see; passive, seem (VIDEBERIS, VIDES, VIDENT).

Third Conjugation

ATTERO, ATTERERE, ATTRIVI, ATTRITUM rub, rub away (ATTRITUS).

DESINO, DESINERE, DESII stop or cease (DESINAS).

DICO, DICERE, DIXI, DICTUM say, speak, tell; imperative DIC (DICERIS).

DILIGO, DILIGERE, DILEXI, DILECTUM select, favor, prize, love (DILIGIS).

DUCO, DUCERE, DUXI, DUCTUM lead; believe or consider (DUCAS, DUCEBAT).

QUAERO, QUAERERE, QUAESIVI, QUAESITUM search for, inquire (QUAERIS).

PANDO, PANDERE, PANDI, PASSUM stretch out, spread out (PANDAS).

PERDO, PERDERE, PERDIDI, PERDITUM destroy, ruin (PERDITUM).

PERFERO, PERFERRE, PERTULI, PERLATUM carry through, endure; imperative PERFER.

REQUIRO, REQUIRERE, REQUISII, REQUISITUM seek, look for (REQUIRET).

VIVO, VIVERE, VIXI, VICTUS live (VIVE).

Third Conjugation IO

FACIO, FACERE, FECI, FACTUM do, make (FACIAS).

FUGIO, FUGERE, FUGI, FUGITUM flee (FUGIT).

QUATIO, QUATERE, QUASSI, QUASSUM shake (QUASSA).

Fourth Conjugation

INEPTIO, INEPTIRE act foolishly, play the fool.

NESCIO, NESCIRE not know, be ignorant.

Irregular Verbs

ADEO, ADIRE, ADII, ADITUS go or come to (ADIBIT).

FIO, FIERI, FACTUS become, happen (FIEBANT).

NOLO, NOLLE, NOLUI be unwilling (NOLEBAT).

PEREO, PERIRE, PERII perish, be ruined (PERISSE).

POSSUM, POSSE, POTUI be able (POSSIT, POSSES, POSSINT).

SUM, ESSE, FUI be (SINT, EST).

VOLO, VELLE, VOLUI want, wish (VELLES, VOLEBAS, VOLT alt VULT).

NOUNS
First Declension

BITHYNIA a Roman province, modern northwestern Turkey.
LECTICA litter.
PUELLA girl.
PROVINCIA province; a large administrative division of the lands conquered by Rome; Bithynia and Northern Italy are the two referred to by Catullus.

Masculine Proper Name: CINNA probably the poet Gaius Helvius Cinna.

Second Declension
Masculine

AMICUS friend.
GAIUS common first name for Roman males.
GRABATUS a Macedonian word for a small bed used in army encampments; army cot.
LOCUS place; neuter in plural LOCA, LOCORUM regions.
NUNTIUS messenger; message, news.
OCULUS eye.
PILUS a hair; NON FACERE ALIQUEM PILI to consider someone not worth a hair, ie a damn.

Persons

CATULLUS the author.
VARUS possibly Quintilius Varus, a prominent intellectual who was later a friend of the poet Horace. He is mentioned in poems 10 and 22; see segment 9.
VERANIUS a friend whom Catullus usually mentions in connection with Fabullus. Veranius and Fabullus evidently travelled to Spain together and later served on the gubernatorial staff of the notorious Piso in Macedonia.

Neuter

COLLUM neck.
FACTUM deed, action; from perfect participle of FACIO (do).
FORUM forum; a public square in a Roman town; the forum in Rome was surrounded by the Curia or senate, the temple of Castor and Pollux and several basilicas, large buildings for public business, trials etc.
SCORTILLUM diminutive of SCORTUM (prostitute).

Third Declension
Liquid Stems (L,R)

AMOR, AMORIS (m) love.
FRATER, FRATRIS (m) brother.
IRRUMATOR, IRRUMATORIS (m) literally one who forces his way in; term of abuse referring to oral sex; pervert.
MATER, MATRIS (f) mother.
PRAETOR, PRAETORIS (m) praetor; after the consuls, praetors were the second highest magistrates in Rome; they conducted courts of law during their terms of office and governed provinces afterwards, like former consuls.

Dental Stems (D,T)

CAPUT, CAPITIS (n) head.
COHORS, COHORTIS (f) company, troop, retinue; the staff of a governor.
PES, PEDIS (m) foot.
PENATES, PENATIUM (m) the Penates, old Latin deities of the household; plural forms only.

Nasal Stems

HOMO, HOMINIS (m) man, person.
NATIO, NATIONIS (f) nation, people.
RATIO, RATIONIS (f) reason; particular plan or rationale or rationality in general; RATIO ME FUGIT reason escaped me, I forgot what I was saying.
SERMO, SERMONIS (m) talk, conversation.

S-STEMS

AES, AERIS (n) copper, bronze, bronze coin, money.
MOS, MORIS (m) habit, custom.
OS, ORIS (n) mouth, face.

I-STEMS

SERAPIS, SERAPIS (m) Egyptian deity identified with Osiris, a god of agriculture and civilization, who was worshipped with his spouse Isis; a popular religion among lower class Romans; acc SERAPIM; alt SARAPIS.
SODALIS, SODALIS (m) comrade, companion.

Fourth Conjugation

ANUS, ANUS (f) old woman.
DOMUS, DOMUS (f) house, home; locative DOMI at home; accusative of direction, VENIRE DOMUM to come home.

ADJECTIVES
First-Second Declension

BEATUS blessed, fortunate; perfect participle of BEO (bless); comp BEATIOR, BEATIUS.

CERTUS certain; adverb CERTE.

CINAEDUS from the Greek word (KINAIDOS) for a passive homosexual; loose, wanton, amoral; comp CINAEDIOR, CINAEDIUS.

ILLEPIDUS not charming, rude, boorish; alt INLEPIDUS.

INSULSUS literally unsalted; insipid, stupid, tasteless, awkward.

INVENUSTUS lacking charm, boorish.

JUCUNDUS pleasant, jolly, gay.

LAETUS happy; comp LAETIOR, LAETIUS.

MALUS bad, evil; adv MALE.

MALIGNUS bad, stingy; adv MALIGNE.

MEUS my, mine.

MOLESTUS annoying, irritating.

OTIOSUS full of OTIUM (leisure); at leisure, unoccupied.

PAULUS little; adv PAULUM a little.

RECTUS straight; the perfect participle of REGO (guide, direct).

SANUS sane, healthy; adv SANE reasonably, doubtlessly.

SUUS his, her, its or their own.

TUUS your, yours (singular).

UNANIMUS of one spirit, harmonious.

UNCTUS sleek, rich; comp UNCTIOR, UNCTIUS; perfect participle of UNGO (to oil or perfume).

VARIUS various, miscellaneous.

VERUS true; adv VERUM, VERE.

Third Declension
I-Stems

OMNIS, OMNE all, every.

INCOLUMIS, INCOLUME safe, unharmed.

One Termination

HIBER (HIBERIS) Iberian, Spanish.

NEGLEGENS (NEGLEGENTIS) negligent; present participle of NEGLEGO.

VETUS (VETERIS) old.

VERBS
First Conjugation

ANTISTO, ANTISTARE, ANTISTETI stand before, excel (ANTISTANS).

APPLICO, APPLICARE place upon, bring one thing near or in contact with another (APPLICANS).

COLLOCO, COLLOCARE arrange in a place, place something somewhere; alt CONLOCO.

COMMODO, COMMODARE adapt to some purpose; loan (COMMODA).

COMPARO, COMPARARE acquire (COMPARAVISTI > COMPARASTI)

NARRO, NARRARE narrate, recount (NARRANTEM).
PARO, PARARE acquire (PARAVERIM > PARARIM, PARAVIT).
SUAVIOR, SUAVIARI, SUAVIATUS kiss; alt SAVIOR (SUAVIABOR).

Second Conjugation

DECET, DECERE, DECUIT impersonal verb, it is becoming or appropriate.
HABEO, HABERE, HABUI, HABITUM have; SE HABERE = to be, feel, get along in a particular way (HABERET).
LICET, LICERE, LICUIT impersonal verb with complementary infinitive; it is permissible to do something.
MANEO, MANERE, MANSI remain, stay (MANE).
RESPONDEO, RESPONDERE, RESPONDI, RESPONSUM answer, respond.
VIDEO, VIDERE, VIDI, VISUM see; passive, seem (VISUM EST).

Third Conjugation

DEFERO, DEFERRE, DETULI, DELATUM carry down, deliver (DEFERRI).
DICO, DICERE, DIXI, DICTUM say, speak, tell (DIXERAM, DICITUR).
DUCO, DUCERE, DUXI, DUCTUM lead (DUXERAT).
FRANGO, FRANGERE, FREGI, FRACTUM break.
INCIDO, INCIDERE, INCIDI fall upon, befall, occur (INCIDERUNT > INCIDERE, INCIDISSET).
NASCOR, NASCI, NATUS be born (NATUM ESSE).
QUAESO, QUAESERE, QUAESIVI, QUAESITUM seek, ask for information or to be given something; archaic form of QUAERO.
REFERO, REFERRE, RETULI, RELATUM bring back (REFERRET).
UTOR, UTI, USUS use; ablative object.
VISO, VISERE, VISI, VISUM view, visit; frequentative of VIDEO (VISAM).
VIVO, VIVERE, VIXI, VICTUM live (VIVIS).

Third Conjugation IO

FACIO, FACERE, FECI, FACTUM do, make; FACTUM as a noun, thing done, deed, action (FACEREM, FACERET, FACTA).
FUGIO, FUGERE, FUGI flee (FUGIT).

Fourth Conjugation

AUDIO, AUDIRE, AUDIVI, AUDITUM to hear, listen (AUDIAM).
VENIO, VENIRE, VENI come (VENIMUS, VENISTI).

Irregular Verbs

INQUAM irregular verb, I say; used for direct quotations; INQUAM and INQUII (first person); INQUIT (third singular); INQUIUNT (third plural).

POSSUM, POSSE, POTUI be able (POSSEM, POSSET).

PROSUM, PRODESSE, PROFUI to be useful or profitable to (PROFUISSET).

SUM, ESSE, FUI be (EST, ESSET, ERAT, FUIT).

VOLO, VELLE, VOLUI want, wish, desire.

NOUNS
First Declension

CULPA guilt.
FACETIAE wit; plural forms only.
PUELLA girl.
UNDA wave.

Second Declension Nouns
Masculine

HENDECASYLLABUS a hendecasyllabic line of verse.
JOCUS joke.
MOECHUS adulterer.
NILUS the Nile river.
RHENUS the Rhine river.

Persons

ASINIUS Gnaeus Asinius Marrucinus, the undistinguished elder
brother of Gaius Asinius Pollio (see POLLIO below).
AURELIUS Furius' comrade and like him a rival for Juventius'
affection.
CATULLUS the author.
FABULLUS a friend of Catullus usually mentioned with Veranius.
FURIUS a friend of Catullus, usually linked with Aurelius;
possibly Marcus Furius Bibaculus, a minor poet. He wrote poems
abusing Caesar early in his career but later composed an epic
celebrating his victories in Gaul. The latter contained the
notorious line {Baehrens Fragmenta Poetarum Romanorum frg.15}:
JUPPITER HIBERNAS CANA NIVE CONSPUIT ALPES ("Jupiter spits on the
winter Alps with hoary snow").
VERANIOLUS little Veranius; diminutive of VERANIUS.
VERANIUS Fabullus' companion.

RUS > R: PUER, PUERI boy.

Neuter

ARATRUM plough.
DICTUM word, saying; perfect participle of DICO (say, tell).
FURTUM theft.
LINTEUM linen, cloth.
MNEMOSYNUM a souvenir; from the Greek word for memory.
MONIMENTUM monument.
PRATUM meadow.
SUDARIUM handkerchief; from SUDOR (sweat).
TALENTUM a talent, a very large unit of money used by the Greeks.
VINUM wine.

Third Declension
Liquid Stems (LR)

AEQUOR, AEQUORIS (n) the flat surface of the sea; the sea.
AMOR, AMORIS (m) love.
FRATER, FRATRIS (m) brother.
LEPOR, LEPORIS (m) charm.

S-Stems

FLOS, FLORIS (m) flower.
LITUS, LITORIS (n) the shore.
MUNUS, MUNERIS (n) gift, duty.

I-Stems

ALPES, ALPIUM (f) the Alps.
ILE, ILIS (n) genitals.
SODALIS, SODALIS (mf) comrade, companion.

Dental Stems (D,T)

COMES, COMITIS (mf) companion.
VOLUNTAS, VOLUNTATIS (f) will, pleasure.

Nasal Stem: AESTIMATIO, AESTIMATIONIS (f) value, worth.

Persons

CAESAR, CAESARIS Gaius Iulius Caesar, the later dictator.
POLLIO, POLLIONIS probably Gaius Asinius Pollio, a famous orator, poet and historian, whose writings have not survived. He was a friend of Caesar, Horace, Vergil; in his fourth eclogue Vergil uses the year of his consulship (40 BC) as the beginning of a golden age.

Fourth Declension: MANUS, MANUS (f) hand.

Fifth Declension: RES, REI (f) thing, affair, situation.

ETHNIC NOMENCLATURE

ARABES (m) the Arabs; ARABAS Greek accusative plural.
BRITANNI the British.
HIBERI the Spaniards.
HYRCANI Hyrcanians, a tribe that lived on the shores of the Caspian sea.
INDI the Indians.
PARTHI the Parthians, another Caspian tribe.
SAGAE (m) the Sagae, a people in southern Russia; a subdivision of the Scythians; alt SACAE.

ADJECTIVES
First-Second Declension

ALTUS high.
BELLUS pretty, fair; adv BELLE.
BONUS good.
DIFFERTUS stuffed, full of; from the perfect participle of FARCIO (fill); Q's reading for DISERTUS at 12.9.
DISERTUS eloquent.
EOUS eastern.
EXTREMUS (superlative of EXTERUS outer) outermost, very far away.
GALLICUS Gallic, French.
INEPTUS foolish, stupid.
INVENUSTUS lacking charm, boorish.
LONGUS long, far; adverb LONGE.
MAGNUS great.
MARRUCINUS Marrucinian, belonging to the Marrucini, a people on the eastern coast of Italy; cognomen of Gnaeus Asinius.
MEUS my, mine.
PAUCUS little; plural PAUCI, PAUCAE, PAUCA few.
SAETABUS of or from Saetabis, a Spanish town, famous for fabrics.
SALSUS salty, witty, clever.
SEPTEMGEMINUS sevenfold.
SORDIDUS sordid, vulgar, dirty.
SUUS his, her, its or their own.
ULTIMUS farthest, most remote.
VERUS true; adv VERE or VERUM.

RUS > ER

SAGITTIFER, SAGITTIFERA, SAGITTIFERUM arrow-bearing.
SINISTER, SINISTRA, SINISTRUM left, on the left side; unfavorable.

Third Declension
I-Stems

HORRIBILIS, HORRIBILE horrible, dreadful.
MOLLIS, MOLLE soft, dainty, effeminate.
OMNIS, OMNE all, every.

One termination

CAELES (CAELITIS) heavenly; as substantative, the heavenly ones, the gods.
NEGLEGENS (NEGLEGENTIS) negligent; comp NEGLEGENTIOR, NEGLEGENTIUS; present participle of NEGLEGO (neglect).

VERBS
First Conjugation

AMO, AMARE love (AMANS, AMEM).
COLORO, COLORARE color (COLORAT).
EXSPECTO, EXSPECTARE await, expect (EXSPECTA).
MUTO, MUTARE change (MUTARI).
NUNTIO, NUNTIARE announce (NUNTIATE).
PARO, PARARE prepare, obtain (PARATI).
PENETRO, PENETRARE to penetrate (PENETRABIT).
PUTO, PUTARE think (PUTAS).
RESONO, RESONARE echo, resound (RESONANTE).
RESPECTO, RESPECTARE look back for or at (RESPECTET).
TEMPTO, TEMPTARE try, attempt.

Second Conjugation

MOVEO, MOVERE, MOVI, MOTUM move (MOVET).
TENEO, TENERE, TENUI, TENTUM hold, keep (TENET).
VALEO, VALERE, VALUI be well or strong, fare well (VALEAT).

Third Conjugation

CADO, CADERE, CECIDI, CASUS fall (CECIDIT).
COMPLECTOR, COMPLECTI, COMPLEXUS embrace (COMPLEXA).
CREDO, CREDERE, CREDIDI, CREDITUM believe (CREDIS, CREDIS).
DICO, DICERE, DIXI, DICTUM say, speak, tell (DICTA).
FERO, FERRE, TULI, LATUM carry, bear (FERET).
MITTO, MITTERE, MISI, MISSUM send (MISERUNT).
REMITTO, REMITTERE, REMISI, REMISSUM return, give back (REMITTE).
RUMPO, RUMPERE, RUPI, RUPTUM break, burst (RUMPENS).
TANGO, TANGERE, TETIGI, TACTUM touch (TACTUS EST).
TOLLO, TOLLERE, SUSTULI, SUBLATUM lift up, remove (TOLLIS).
TUNDO, TUNDERE, TUTUDI, TUSUM strike, beat (TUNDITUR).
VISO, VISERE, VISI, VISUM view, visit; frequentative of VIDEO (VISENS).
VIVO, VIVERE, VIXI, VICTUM live (VIVAT).
UTOR, UTI, USUS use; ablative object (UTERIS).

Third Conjugation IO

FUGIO, FUGERE, FUGI flee, escape (FUGIT).
GRADIOR, GRADI, GRESSUS go, proceed (GRADIETUR).

Irregular Verbs

PRAETEREO, PRAETERIRE, PRAETERIVI, PRAETERITUM go by, pass (PRAETEREUNTE).
SUM, ESSE, FUI be (EST).
VOLO, VELLE, VOLUI wish, be willing, desire (VELIT).

NOUNS
First Declension
Feminine

ARANEA spider; spider's web.
CENA dinner.
INEPTIAE foolishness, stupidity; plural forms only.
PUELLA girl.

Masculine

POETA poet.
SULLA possibly Cornelius Epicadus Sulla, a freedman of the famous Sulla.

Second Declension
Masculine

CACHINNUS laughter.
DEUS god (nom. pl. DI; gen. pl. DEORUM or DEUM; dat. and abl. plural DIIS or DIS).
LIBRARIUS a person who works with books; scribe, bookdealer.
LIBELLUS booklet, diminutive of LIBER.
NASUS nose.
OCULUS eye.
SACCULUS little bag; wallet, purse.

Persons

AQUINUS Possibly the poet Aquinius of whom Cicero wrote (Tusculan Disputations V.63): "I never knew a poet who did not consider himself excellent -- and I knew Aquinius."
CAESIUS a poet despised by Catullus.
CALVUS Gaius Licinius Calvus ("The Bald") Macer ("The Lean"), a friend of Catullus and prominent poet and orator. His best known poem seems to have been a miniature epic or epyllion on the sufferings of Io, the girl who was loved by Jupiter and driven around the world in the shape of a cow because of Juno's jealousy. Its most famous line {Baehrens _Fragmenta Poetarum Romanorum_ frg.9}: A VIRGO INFELIX HERBIS PASCERIS AMARIS ("Alas, poor girl, you will graze on bitter grass.")
CATULLUS the author.
FABULLUS Catullus' friend; see segment 5.
SUFFENUS a conceited poet, ridiculed in 22.

NEUTER

ODIUM hatred.
SAECLUM age, generation.

SCRINIUM case or chest for keeping books; bookshelf.
SUPPLICIUM punishment, torture.
UNGUENTUM perfume, ointment.
VENENUM poison.
VINUM wine.

Third Declension
Liquid Stems (L,R)

AMOR, AMORIS (m) love.
LABOR, LABORIS (m) work, labor.
LECTOR, LECTORIS (m) reader.
LITTERATOR, LITTERATORIS (m) a teacher of reading and writing, an elementary teacher; a grammarian.
SAL, SALIS (m) salt; used figuratively to mean wit.

Dental Stems (D,T)

CLIENS, CLIENTIS (m) client; a man of moderate or low income who courted the favor of a wealthy PATRONUS (patron) and depended on him for legal assistance and other favors.
FORS, FORTIS (f) chance, luck; adv FORTE by chance.
PES, PEDIS (m) foot.

S-Stems

MUNUS, MUNERIS (n) gift, duty.
VENUS, VENERIS (f) Venus, the goddess of love.

N-Stem: CUPIDO, CUPIDINIS (m) Cupid.

Fourth Declension: MANUS, MANUS (f) hand.

Fifth Declension: DIES, DIEI (mf) day.

ADJECTIVES
First-Second Declension

BEATUS blessed, fortunate; perfect participle of BEO (bless); comp BEATIOR, BEATIUS.
BONUS good.
CANDIDUS bright.
CONTINUUS continuous, following, next.
FALSUS wrong, mistaken; false, deceitful; perfect participle of FALLO (cheat, deceive).
INCOMMODUS inconvenient, annoying; neuter as a noun, disadvantage, trouble.
IMPIUS impious, faithless, disloyal.
JUCUNDUS pleasant, jolly, gay; superlative JUCUNDISSIMUS.

MAGNUS great.

MALUS bad, evil; adverb MALE.

MERUS pure, often of wine that has not been diluted with water.

MEUS my, mine.

MULTUS much, many.

NOVUS new, strange.

OPTIMUS best; superlative of BONUS.

PAUCUS little; plural PAUCI, PAUCAE, PAUCA few.

PESSIMUS worst; superlative of MALUS.

PLENUS full, full of (with genitive).

SALSUS salted, witty; perfect participle of SALIO; SALSE is Quinn's emendation in 14.16; other editors have FALSE.

TUUS your, yours.

VATINIANUS Vatinian, of or like Vatinius, a politician who supported Julius Caesar and was prosecuted by Catullus' friend, Calvus, on several occasions; see segment 19.

VENUSTUS charming, beautiful.

-RUS > -(E)R

NOSTER, NOSTRA, NOSTRUM our, ours.

SACER, SACRA, SACRUM sacred, holy; also in a bad sense, cursed, detestable.

VESTRA, VESTRA, VESTRUM your, yours.

Third Declension
I-Stems

HORRIBILIS, HORRIBILE horrible, frightening.

OMNIS, OMNE all, every.

SATURNALIS, SATURNALE having to do with Saturn; neuter plural as a substantive, SATURNALIA, the festival of Saturn, the latter part of December devoted to festivities in honor of Saturn, similar to the modern holiday season.

SUAVIS, SUAVE sweet, agreeable; comp SUAVIOR, SUAVIUS.

One Termination

ELEGANS (ELEGANTIS) elegant; comp ELEGANTIOR, ELEGANTIUS.

PLUS more; in the singular only in the neuter accusative/adverbial form PLUS; plural forms: PLURES, PLURA etc.

VERBS
First Conjugation

AMO, AMARE love (AMAREM).

CENO, CENARE dine (CENABIS).

DO, DARE, DEDI, DATUM, give (DABO, DAT, DENT).

DONO, DONARE give, dedicate, bestow; emphatic form of DO (DONAVERUNT > DONARUNT).

REMUNEROR, REMUNERARI, REMUNERATUS pay back, remunerate

39

(REMUNERABOR).
ROGO, ROGARE ask, ask for something (ROGABIS).
SUSPICOR, SUSPICARI, SUSPICATUS suspect, conjecture.

Second Conjugation

ADMOVEO, ADMOVERE, ADMOVI, ADMOTUM move to or towards, apply.
FAVEO, FAVERE, FAVI, FAUTUM favor, be favorable to; dative object
(FAVENT).
HORREO, HORRERE, HORRUI bristle, shudder, shudder to do something
(HORREBITIS).
LUCEO, LUCERE, LUXI shine, be bright; third person used
impersonally of daylight: LUCET it is light (LUXERIT).
VALEO, VALERE, VALUI be well or strong; imperatives VALE and
VALETE = farewell.

Third Conjugation

ADFERO, ADFERRE, ATTULI, ADLATUM carry or bring to or near
(ATTULISTIS, ATTULERIS, ATTULISTIS).
COLLIGO, COLLIGERE, COLLEGI, COLLECTUM collect, gather together
(COLLIGAM).
CURRO, CURRERE, CUCURRI run (CURRAM).
LOQUOR, LOQUI, LOCUTUS say, speak, tell (LOCUTUS SUM).
MITTO, MITTERE, MISI, MISSUM send (MISIT, MISISTI > MISTI).
PERDO, PERDERE, PERDIDI, PERDITUM, destroy, ruin (PERDERES).

Third Conjugation IO

ACCIPIO, ACCIPERE, ACCEPI, ACCEPTUM receive, accept (ACCIPIES).
FACIO, FACERE, FECI, FACTUM do, make (FACIANT).
OLFACIO, OLFACERE, OLFECI, OLFACTUM smell, detect by smelling
(OLFACIES).

Fourth Conjugation

REPERIO, REPERIRE, REPPERI, REPERTUM find, discover, invent;
NOVUM ET REPERTUM hendiadyes for "newly invented".

Irregular Verbs

ABEO, ABIRE, ABII go away; come off in the sense of succeed or
work out (ABITE, ABIBIT).
DISPEREO, DISPERIRE, DISPERII perish; intensive of PEREO
(DISPEREUNT).
ODI hate (ODISSEM).
PEREO, PERIRE, PERII perish (PERIRET).
SUM, ESSE, FUI be (ERITIS).

NOUNS
First Declension
Feminine

CULPA guilt.
INSIDIAE, INSIDIARUM treachery, deceit; plural forms only.
PLATEA street.
PORTA gate.
VENIA grace, favor.

Masculine: POETA poet.

SECOND DECLENSION
Masculine

ANIMUS soul, spirit.
LUMBUS male genitals, usually plural.
POPULUS people.
RAPHANUS radish.
VERSICULUS little verse; diminutive of VERSUS.

Persons

AURELIUS Furius' comrade; see segment 5.
FURIUS a friend of Catullus; see segments 5 and 10.

RUS > R: PUER, PUERI boy.

NEUTER

BASIUM kiss.
FATUM fate.
PARUM indeclinable noun, a little; adv "scarcely."

Third Declension
Dental Stems (D,T)

CAPUT, CAPITIS (n) head.
MENS, MENTIS (f) mind.
PES, PEDIS (m) foot.

Liquid Stems (L,R)

AMOR, AMORIS (m) love.
FUROR, FURORIS (m) madness, fury.
LEPOR, LEPORIS (m) charm.
SAL, SALIS (m) salt; figuratively, wit.

FORIS, FORIS (f) door; adverb FORIS outdoors, outside (= ablataive of older nominative singular FORA).
MUGILIS, MUGILIS (m) mullet, a fish supposedly used in a punishment for adultery; see appendix.
PENIS, PENIS (m) penis.

Fifth Declension: RES, REI (f) thing, affair, situation.

ADJECTIVES
First-Second Declension

BONUS good.
CASTUS chaste, pure.
CINAEDUS loose, wanton, amoral.
DURUS hard.
INFESTUS hostile, dangerous.
INTEGELLUS pure or chaste (little); diminutive of INTEGER (pure).
MALUS bad, evil; adverb MALE.
MEUS my, mine.
MOLLICULUS soft or gentle (little); diminutive of MOLLIS.
MULTUS much, many.
PATHICUS pathic, passively homosexual.
PILOSUS hairy; full of PILI (hairs).
PIUS pious, loyal.
PUDICUS modest, proper, chaste; adverb PUDICE.
SCELESTUS depraved, immoral; characterized by SCELUS (crime).
SUUS his, her, its or their own.
TUUS your, yours.
VERUS true; adv. VERE, VERUM.

RUS > (E)R

MISER, MISERA, MISERUM miserable.
NOSTER, NOSTRA, NOSTRUM our, ours.

Third Declension
One Termination

MAS (MARIS) male, masculine.
PUDENS (PUDENTIS) proper, modest; adv PUDENTER.
VECORS (VECORDIS) mad, insane.

Indeclinable: NECESSE necessary.

VERBS
First Conjugation

COMMENDO, COMMENDARE to commit or entrust to someone's care.
CONSERVO, CONSERVARE protect; keep (CONSERVES).

42

INCITO, INCITARE rouse up, incite.
IRRUMO, IRRUMARE force one's way in; obscene term referring to oral sex.
LACESSO, LACESSARE bother, annoy, irritate (LACESSAS).
OCCUPO, OCCUPARE seize, take possession of, occupy (OCCUPATI).
PARO, PARARE prepare, obtain (PARATUM ERIT).
PEDICO, PEDICARE assault sexually, of an aggressive homosexual male (PEDICABO).
PUTO, PUTARE think (PUTATIS, PUTAVISTIS > PUTASTIS).

Second Conjugation

DECET, DECERE, DECUIT impersonal verb, it is becoming or appropriate.
HABEO, HABERE, HABUI, HABITUM have (HABENT).
LUBET, LUBERE impersonal verb, it is pleasing; alt LIBET.
MOVEO, MOVERE, MOVI, MOTUM move (MOVETO).
PATEO, PATERE, PATUI lie or be open (PATENTE).
VEREOR, VERERI, VERITUM fear (VEREMUR).

Third Conjugation

ATTRAHO, ATTRAHERE, ATTRAXI, ATTRACTUM draw or pull up to a place or into position; the ablative absolute PEDIBUS ATTRACTIS (feet pulled up) was commonly used to describe the position of the inferior partner in sexual intercourse or similar activity. An obscene graffito from Pompeii (CORPUS INSCRIPTIONUM LATINARUM IV, 1261) reads (with its spelling corrected) FUTUEBATUR -- FUTUEBATUR, INQUAM, CIVIUM ROMANORUM, ATTRACTIS PEDIBUS, CUNNUS IN QUA NULLAE ALIAE VICES ERANT NISI DULCISSIMAE ET PIISSIMAE.
DICO, DICERE, DIXI, DICTUM say, speak, tell.
EXPETO, EXPETERE, EXPETII, EXPETITUM seek after, strive for; strive to do or have something (EXPETERES).
IMPELLO, IMPELLERE, IMPULI, IMPULSUM to strike; to force or impel somewhere or into doing something (IMPULERIT).
LEGO, LEGERE, LEGI, LECTUM collect, gather; gather words, hence read -- its principal meaning in Catullus (LEGISTIS).
METUO, METUERE, METUI, METUTUM fear.
PERCURRO, PERCURRERE, PERCUCURRI run through (PERCURRENT).
PETO, PETERE, PETII, PETITUM seek.

Third Conjugation IO

CUPIO, CUPERE, CUPII, CUPITUM desire (CUPISTI).
EXCIPIO, EXCIPERE, EXCEPI, EXCEPTUM except, make an exception of.

Fourth Conjugation: PRURIO, PRURIRE, PRURIVI itch (PRURIAT).

Irregular Verbs

NEQUEO, NEQUIRE, NEQUIVI to be unable (NEQUEUNT).
POSSUM, POSSE, POTUI be able (POSSUNT).
PRAETEREO, PRAETERIRE, PRAETERIVI, PRAETERITUM go by, pass
(PRAETEREUNT).
SUM, ESSE, FUI am, be (ERIT, SUNT, EST).
VOLO, VELLE, VOLUI want, wish, desire (VIS).

Appendix

In poem 15, Catullus alludes to one of classical antiquity's
strangest traditions: that men caught committing adultery or
similar crimes (like seducing Juventius) should be punished by
having their buttocks singed and radishes inserted into their
rectums. The principal evidence for this custom is line 1083 in
The Clouds by Aristophanes with its ancient anonymous footnote
or "scholion." In the passage involved, Unjust Logic explains
how adultery can be justified by reference to Zeus' amours. Just
Logic replies, "What if a person takes your advice and ends up
radished and singed?" The scholion reads: "This is how
adulterers were punished. People inserted radishes into their
rectums and sprinkled hot ashes on them until a sufficient degree
of torture had been achieved." The addition of fish to recipe is
mentioned only by Catullus and his fellow Roman Juvenal (10.317).
Whether or how often this punishment was actually inflicted is
anybody's guess. Its existence, however, if only as a threat,
must have had a salutary effect on morality.

SEGMENT 8 (Poems 17 & 21)

NOUNS
First Declension

AXULA splinter of wood; diminutive of AXIS (axle); alt ASSULA.
COLONIA colony, colonial town or settlement.
FOSSA trench, ditch.
INSIDIAE, INSIDIARUM treachery, deceit; plural forms only.
MULA mule.
PUELLA girl.
SOLEA sandal.
ULNA elbow.
UVA bunch of grapes.

SECOND DECLENSION
Masculine

ANIMUS soul, spirit.
ANNUS year.
HAEDUS kid, young goat.
PILUS a hair; NON FACERE PILI consider worthless.
PONTICULUS little bridge; diminutive of PONS.
SALISUBSULUS comical name for Mars coined by Catullus with reference to the SALII or "Jumpers," priests of Mars, and the verb SUBSILIO (jump up).

Person: AURELIUS Furius' comrade; see segment 5.

RUS > R: PUER, PUERI boy.

Feminine: ALNUS alder tree.

NEUTER

CAENUM filth.
LUTUM mud.

Third Declension
Dental Stems (D,T)

CAPUT, CAPITIS (n) head.
PALUS, PALUDIS (f) swamp.
PARS, PARTIS (f) part.
PES, PEDIS (m) foot.
PONS, PONTIS (m) bridge.

Nasal Stems

ESURITIO, ESURITIONIS (f) hunger, famine.
HOMO, HOMINIS (m) man, person.

45

IRRUMATIO, IRRUMATIONIS (f) forced entry, referring to oral sex.
LIBIDO, LIBIDINIS (f) desire, passion.
VORAGO, VORAGINIS (f) pit, hole, chasm.

S-Stems

CRUS, CRURIS (n) shin, leg.
FLOS, FLORIS (m) flower.
LATUS, LATERIS (n) side, hip, thigh.
MUNUS, MUNERIS (n) gift, duty.

Liquid Stems (L,R)

AMOR, AMORIS (m) love; plural used as a term of endearment.
INSTAR (n) nominative and accusative only; image, equivalent;
with genitive = "like."
PATER, PATRIS (m) father.
STUPOR, STUPORIS (m) dullness, stupidity, stupor.

I-Stems

FINIS, FINIS (m) end, limit, boundary.
SECURIS, SECURIS (f) ax, hatchet; ablative SECURI.

Labial Stem (B,P): MUNICEPS, MUNICIPIS (m) townsman.

Fourth Declension

LACUS, LACUS (m) lake.
RISUS, RISUS (m) laugh, laughter.

ADJECTIVES
First-Second Declension

BIMULUS (little) two-year-old; diminutive of BIMUS.
BONUS good.
CAVUS hollow.
DELICATUS delicate, dainty; comp DELICATIOR.
FERREUS iron.
INEPTUS foolish, stupid; adverb INEPTE.
INSULSUS unsalted; insipid, stupid; superl INSULSISSIMUS.
LIVIDUS livid, black and blue; dark and dull in color;
superlative LIVIDISSIMUS.
LONGUS long, far; adverb LONGE.
MAXIMUS greatest, most; superlative of MAGNUS; adverb MAXIME.
MEUS my, mine.
PROFUNDUS deep.
PRONUS prone, leaning forward or lying on the stomach; cp
SUPINUS.
PUDICUS modest, proper, chaste; adverb PUDICE.
PUTIDUS rotten.

REDIVIVUS living again; secondhand, reused.
STOLIDUS stolid, dull, insensitive.
SUPINUS supine, leaning or lying back, inactive; cp PRONUS.
SUPPERNATUS lame or wounded in the hip (PERNA) or leg.
SUUS his, her, its or their own.
TENELLULUS tender (little); dimin. of TENER (tender, delicate).
TREMULUS shaky, tremulous.
TUUS your, yours.
VERUS true; adv VERUM, VERE.
VETERNUS old.

-RUS > (E)R

NIGER, NIGRA, NIGRUM black, dark; superlative NIGERRIMUS.
SACER, SACRA, SACRUM sacred, holy.
SATUR, SATURA, SATURUM full, full of food, satisfied.

Third Declension
I-Stems

GRAVIS, GRAVE heavy, serious.
OMNIS, OMNE all, every.
POTIS, POTE able, capable; POTE = POTE EST (it is possible).
VIRIDIS, VIRIDE green, fresh; superlative VIRIDISSIMUS.

One Termination

DILIGENS (DILIGENTIS) diligent, energetic; comp DILIGENTIOR.
LIGUR (LIGURIS) Ligurian, from Liguria, the area of Genoa.
PRAECEPS (PRAECIPITIS) headfirst, headlong.
TENAX (TENACIS) tenacious, clinging, tending to hold.

Irregular comparative: PRIOR, PRIUS, prior, previous; adv PRIUS.

VERBS
First Conjugation

ADSERVO, ADSERVARE guard, preserve (ADSERVANDA).
DO, DARE, DEDI, DATUM give (DA).
EXCITO, EXCITARE excite, arouse.
IRRUMO, IRRUMARE enter by force; obscene term referring to oral sex.
JOCOR, JOCARI, JOCATUS joke (JOCARIS).
PARO, PARARE prepare, obtain (PARATUM HABES = PARAVISTI).
PEDICO, PEDICARE assault sexually, of an aggressive homosexual.
STO, STARE, STETI stand (STANTIS).
SUBLEVO, SUBLEVARE lift up (SUBLEVAT).

Second Conjugation

DOLEO, DOLERE, DOLUI suffer, feel sorry, grieve.

47

HABEO, HABERE, HABUI, HABITUM have (HABES).
HAEREO, HAERERE, HAESI, HAESUM cling to, adhere to (HAERENS).
JACEO, JACERE, JACUI lie, recline (JACET).
LICET, LICERE, LICUIT impersonal verb; it is permissible (to do).
LUBET, LUBERE, LUBUIT impersonal verb, it is pleasing; alt LIBET.
TACEO, TACERE, TACUI be silent (TACEREM).
VEREOR, VERERI, VERITUS fear (VERERIS).
VIDEO, VIDERE, VIDI, VISUM see; passive, seem (VIDET).

Third Conjugation

DERELINQUO, DERELINQUERE, DERELIQUI, DERELICTUM leave, abandon.
DESINO, DESINERE, DESII stop or cease, with infinitive (DESINE).
DISCO, DISCERE, DIDICI learn (DISCET).
INSTRUO, INSTRUERE, INSTRUXI, INSTRUCTUM pile up, build up,
construct (INSTRUENTEM).
LUDO, LUDERE, LUSI, LUSUM play, mock.
MITTO, MITTERE, MISI, MISSUM send.
NUBO, NUBERE, NUPSI, NUPTUM marry someone {dative} (NUPTA SIT).
RECUMBO, RECUMBERE, RECUBUI lie back, recline (RECUMBAT).
SINO, SINERE, SIVI, SITUM allow, permit, leave alone (SINIT).
TANGO, TANGERE, TETIGI, TACTUM touch (TANGAM).

Third Conjugation IO

CUPIO, CUPERE, CUPII, CUPITUM desire (CUPIS).
FACIO, FACERE, FECI, FACTUM do, make (FACIT, FACERES, FACIAS).
SAPIO, SAPERE to have taste, to be wise or sensible (SAPIT).
SUSCIPIO, SUSCIPERE, SUSCEPI, SUSCEPTUM undertake, do, perform
(SUSCIPIANTUR).

Fourth Conjugation

AUDIO, AUDIRE hear, listen (AUDIT).
DORMIO, DORMIRE sleep (DORMIENTIS).
ESURIO, ESURIRE be hungry.
EXPERIOR, EXPERIRI, EXPERTUS try, attempt, test (EXPERIRIS).
NESCIO, NESCIRE not know, be ignorant (NESCIT).
SALIO, SALIRE jump, leap.
SENTIO, SENTIRE, SENSI, SENSUM sense, perceive (SENTIENS).
SITIO, SITIRE be thirsty.

Irregular Verbs

EO, IRE, II go (IRE, EAT).
FIO, FIERI, FACTUS, become, happen (FIAT).
SUM, ESSE, FUI be (ES, EST, SUNT, SIT, ERUNT, FUERUNT).
VOLO, VELLE, VOLUI want, wish, be willing.

NOUNS
First Declension
Feminine

ARCA chest, money box.
CARTA scroll, page; alt CHARTA.
FABA bean.
MANTICA knapsack, leather bag.
MEMBRANA skin; hide prepared for writing, hence parchment.
NOVERCA step-mother.
PITUITA slime, phlegm.
RUINA collapse, falling down; probably used with reference to the fact that cheaply constructed apartment buildings in Rome often collapsed.
SALIVA saliva.

Masculine: SCURRA a wit, a comedian.

SECOND DECLENSION
Masculine

ANNUS year.
ARANEUS spider.
CAPRIMULGUS goat-milker, a humorous term for a peasant.
CULUS "posterior," butt.
DIGITUS finger.
DOLUS trick, trap.
LAPILLUS pebble, diminutive of LAPIDUS (stone).
MUCUS mucus.
NASUS nose.
PALIMPSESTUS a palimpsest, a recycled sheet of papyrus.
SALILLUM little saltshaker; diminutive of SALINUM (SALINULUM > SALILLUM).
SERVUS slave, servant.
UMBILICUS navel, middle; in scrolls, the metal rods that the papyrus or parchment was wound around.

-RUS > -ER: LIBER, LIBRI (m) book.

Persons

FURIUS Marcus Furius Bibaculus; see segments 5 and 10.
SUFFENUS the conceited poet of poem 22; nothing else is known of him.
VARUS mentioned in poems 10 and 22 is possibly Quintilius Varus of Cremona, a prominent intellectual also mentioned by Horace and Vergil. As in Catullus 22, Horace's reference to him in _Ars Poetica_ 438 ff associates him with criticism of most poets'

inability to view their work objectively: "If you recited your poetry to Quintilius, he'd say 'You must change this and improve that and that.' If you said you could do no better, even though you had tried repeatedly, he would tell you take the whole flawed passage back to the anvil. But if you tried to defend your mistake, instead of changing it, he wasted no further word or effort. He just left you alone to enjoy your 'unrivaled love' of yourself and your art."

NEUTER

FACTUM deed; perfect participle of FACIO (make, do).
FURTUM theft.
INCENDIUM fire, conflagration.
LORUM strap, thong of leather.
PERICULUM danger.
PLUMBUM lead; piece of lead.
SESTERTIUM one thousand sesterces, a basic monetary unit in large transactions; a single sesterce was worth approximately one inflated U.S. dollar; see general vocabulary.
TERGUM back.
VENENUM poison.

Third Declension
Liquid Stems (L,R)

ERROR, ERRORIS (m) mistake, foible.
FOSSOR, FOSSORIS (m) ditch-digger.
FRIGOR, FRIGORIS (m) cold.
PATER, PATRIS (m) father.
SOL, SOLIS (m) sun.
SUDOR, SUDORIS (m) sweat.

Palatal Stems (C,G)

CIMEX, CIMICIS (m) bug.
CONJUNX, CONJUGIS (mf) spouse, husband or wife.
PUMEX, PUMICIS (m) pumice stone.
SILEX, SILICIS (mf) flint.

Dental Stems (D,T)

DENS, DENTIS (m) tooth.
PARENS, PARENTIS (mf) parent.
POEMA, POEMATIS (n) poem.

Nasal Stems (N,M)

ESURITIO, ESURITIONIS (f) hunger, famine.
HOMO, HOMINIS (m) man, person.

50

S-Stems

CORPUS, CORPORIS (n) body.
RUS, RURIS (n) field, the countryside.

I-Stem: IGNIS, IGNIS (m) fire.

Fourth Declension

CASUS, CASUS (m) incident, instance, accident; from CADO (fall).
CORNU, CORNUS (n) horn.
MANUS, MANUS (f) hand.
VERSUS, VERSUS (m) verse, line of poetry.

Fifth Declension

MUNDITIES, MUNDITIEI (f) cleanliness, elegance.
RES, REI (f) thing.

ADJECTIVES
First-Second Declension

AEQUUS even, equal; adv AEQUE.
ARIDUS dry, arid.
BEATUS blessed, fortunate; perfect participle BEO (bless); in
Merrill BEATU'S = BEATUS ES; comp BEATIOR, BEATIUS; vocative
BEATE.
BELLUS pretty, fair; adv, BELLE.
COMMODUS convenient.
DURUS hard; comp DURIOR, DURIUS.
IMPIUS impious, faithless, disloyal.
INFACETUS lacking wit, unsophisticated, boorish; comp INFACETIOR,
INFACETIUS.
LIGNEUS wooden; from LIGNUM (piece of wood).
LONGUS long, far; adv LONGE.
MALUS bad.
MIRUS marvellous, surprising.
MUNDUS neat, clean, elegant; comp MUNDIOR, MUNDIUS.
NOVUS new, strange, superlative NOVISSIMUS latest, most recent.
PARVUS small.
PLURIMUS very much, very many, most; superlative of MULTUS.
PROBUS good, proper; adv PROBE well.
PURUS pure, clean; comp PURIOR, PURIUS.
REGIUS royal, regal.
SICCUS dry; comp SICCIOR, SICCIUS.
SUUS his, her, its or their own.
TRITUS polished, smooth, sophisticated; the perfect participle of
TERO (rub, polish); comp TRITIOR, TRITIUS.
TUUS your, yours.
URBANUS urbane; of or from the city.

VENUSTUS charming, beautiful.
VERUS true; adv VERUM, VERE.

-RUS > -(E)R

PULCHER, PULCHRA, PULCHRUM beautiful; adv PULCRE or PULCHRE.
RUBER, RUBRA, RUBRUM red.

Third Declension
I-Stems

GRAVIS, GRAVE heavy, serious.
OMNIS, OMNE all, every.

One Termination

DICAX (DICACIS) talkative.
PLUS more; in the singular only the neuter accusative/adverbial form PLUS; plural forms: PLURES, PLURA etc.

VERBS
First Conjugation

AEQUO, AEQUARE make even or equal (AEQUATA).
CACO, CACARE "relieve oneself" (CACAS).
FRICO, FRICARE, FRICUI, FRICTUM rub (FRICES).
INQUINO, INQUINARE make something dirty, defile.
MIROR, MIRARI, MIRATUS marvel at, admire (MIRATUR).
MUTO, MUTARE to change (MUTAT).
PRECOR, PRECARI, PRECATUS pray; pray for, beg.
PUTO, PUTARE think (PUTEMUS).

Second Conjugation

ABHORREO, ABHORRERE, ABHORRUI shrink away from; be inconsistent with or differ from (ABHORRET).
GAUDEO, GAUDERE, GAUVISUS rejoice, be pleased (GAUDET).
HABEO, HABERE, HABUI, HABITUM have (HABETIS).
SOLEO, SOLERE, SOLITUS be accustomed or wont to do (SOLES).
TIMEO, TIMERE, TIMUI fear (TIMETIS).
VALEO, VALERE, VALUI be well or strong, flourish (VALETIS).
VIDEO, VIDERE, VIDI, VISUM see; passive, seem (VIDEBATUR, VIDEMUS, VIDETUR).

Third Conjugation

ADDO, ADDERE, ADDIDI, ADDITUM add (ADDE).
ATTINGO, ATTINGERE, ATTIGI, ATTACTUM touch (ATTIGIT).
ATTRIBUO, ATTRIBUERE, ATTRIBUI, ATTRIBUTUM allocate, assign, attribute (ATTRIBUTUS EST).
CONCOQUO, CONCOQUERE, CONCOXI, CONCOCTUM literally, cook

together; digest (CONCOQUITIS).
DERIGO, DERIGERE, DEREXI, DERECTUM straighten (DERECTA).
DESINO, DESINERE, DESII stop, cease (DESINE).
FALLO, FALLERE, FALSI, FALSUM deceive, trick (FALLIMUR).
LEGO, LEGERE, LEGI, LECTUM collect, gather; gather words, hence read -- its principal meaning in Catullus (LEGAS).
NOSCO, NOSCERE, NOVI, NOTUS get to know; perfect, know (NOVISTI > NOSTI).
PERSCRIBO, PERSCRIBERE, PERSCRIPSI, PERSCRIPTUM write in full or at length; fill with writing (PERSCRIPTA).
REFERO, REFERRE, RETULI, RELATUM bring back; transmit, report (RELATA).
SCRIBO, SCRIBERE, SCRIPSI, SCRIPTUM write (SCRIBIT).
SPERNO, SPERNERE, SPREVI, SPRETUM reject, scorn.
TERO, TERERE, TRIVI, TRITUM rub, smooth (TERAS).

Third Conjugation IO: FACIO, FACERE, FECI, FACTUM make, do (FACIT, FACTA).

Irregular Verbs

ABSUM, ABESSE, AFUI be away, be absent (ABEST).
COMEDO, COMESSE, COMEDI, COMESUM eat up, devour.
FIO, FIERI, FACTUM become, happen (FIT).
NOLO, NOLLE, NOLUI be unwilling; NOLI + infinitive: don't ---!
POSSUM, POSSE, POTUI be able (POSSUNT, POSSES, POSSIS).
SUM, ESSE, FUI be (EST, SIT).

Appendix

In poem 22 Catullus alludes to an Aesopic fable about knapsacks. The Roman author Phaedrus transmits a version of this, which is given in Latin by Quinn and cited by Merrill. It is translated as follows: "Jupiter placed two knapsacks on each of us. He placed one, which was filled with our own faults, behind our backs; the other, which was weighed down with the faults of others, he hung in front of our chests. For this reason we are not able to see our own faults, but as soon as others err, we turn into critics."

SEGMENT 10 (Poems 24-28)

NOUNS
First Declension
Feminine

ARCA chest, money box.
DEA goddess.
DIVITIAE wealth, plural forms only.
LYMPHA water.
MAGISTRA mistress.
PROCELLA storm, hurricane.
TABULA board, plank; writing tablet.
VAPPA stale wine; as a term of abuse, worthless man, bum.
VERPA vulgar term of abuse referring to male genitals, "prick".

Diminutives

MEDULLULA little marrow; cp MEDULLA (marrow, innermost part).
ORICILLA little ear; cp AURIS; alt AURICILLA.
SARCINULA little pack or bundle; cp SARCINA.
VILLULA little villa, wealthy country home; cp VILLA.

Persons

MURCIA goddess of sloth; Quinn's emendation of MULIER in 25.5.
POSTUMIA an unknown woman, Catullus' drinking companion.

SECOND DECLENSION
Masculine

AMICUS friend.
ANNUS year.
CAPILLUS hair.
CATAGRAPHUS drawing; a Greek word.
CUNICULUS rabbit.
DEUS god (nom pl DI; gen DEORUM / DEUM; dat-abl DIIS / DIS).
FAVONIUS the west wind, Zephyrus.
FLOSCULUS blossom, little flower; diminutive of FLOS.
SERVUS slave, servant.
VENTUS wind.

Persons

FABULLUS friend of Catullus usually mentioned with Veranius with
whom he probably travelled to Macedonia under Piso in 57 ; see
segment 4.
FURIUS probably the poet M. Furius Bibaculus. In poem 26, Furius
is about to lose his villa because of his debts -- according to
Catullus.   One of Furius' two surviving poems ridicules another
man of letters, the grammarian Valerius Cato, for losing his

54

villa. Quinn gives the Latin text. It can be translated as follows. "Just now, Gallus, a banker was taking bids/ throughout the city on Cato's Tusculan villa./ We marvelled that a unique teacher,/ a top-ranked grammarian and excellent poet/ could settle all literary disputes/ but was unable to take care of a single title." Catullus addresses Valerius Cato in poem 56. On Cato, see segment 21; on Furius, segment 5.

IUVENTIUS the youth loved by Catullus and also involved with Furius and Aurelius; nothing further is known of him with certainty.

MEMMIUS Gaius Memmius, a influential politician and minor poet with a well documented career in politics. He was a praetor in 58 and the propraetor or governor of Bithynia in 57/56 when Catullus served on his staff.

REMUS Romulus' brother.

ROMULUS the legendary founder of the city of Rome.

THALLUS possibly Antonius Thallus, a Greek poet from Miletus. Five of his poems survive in the Palatine Anthology, a collection of short Greek poems, and are consistent with the delicacy that Catullus imputes to his Thallus, e.g. book 9, poem 220: "See how the green plane tree extends its sacred foliage to conceal the lovers' mysteries. About its branches hang clusters of sweet grapes, dear to the seasons. Grow on, O plane tree! and may your leaves always shelter devotees of Venus."

THYONIANUS an alternative name for Bacchus or Dionysus from the woman's name, Thyone, the mother of Dionysus in one of his many reincarnations in late mythology.

VERANIUS Fabullus' companion in Spain and Macedonia; see segment 4.

-RUS > (E)R

ARBITER, ARBITRI witness, judge; Q's emendation of ARIES in 25.5.
AUSTER, AUSTRI the south wind.
MINISTER, MINISTRI servant, attendant.
PUER, PUERI boy.

NEUTER

ACINUM berry.
EXPENSUM expense; passive participle of EXPENDO (weigh out).
FLAGELLUM whip, scourge.
LATUSCULUM little side, hip, thigh; diminutive of LATUS.
LUCELLUM small profit; diminutive of LUCRUM (gain).
OPPROBRIUM insult, abuse.
PALLIUM cloak, mantle.
SUDARIUM handkerchief; from SUDOR (sweat).
VINUM wine.

Third Declension
I-Stems

FAMES, FAMIS (f) hunger.
MARE, MARIS (n) sea.
NAVIS, NAVIS (f) ship.
PENIS, PENIS (m) penis.
SENEX, SENIS, (m) an old man.
UNGUIS, UNGUIS (f) claw, talon, fingernail.

Liquid Stems (L,R)

ANSER, ANSERIS (m) goose.
FRIGOR, FRIGORIS (m) cold.
MULIER, MULIERIS (f) woman.
PRAETOR, PRAETORIS (m) praetor; after the consuls, praetors were the second highest magistrates in Rome; they conducted courts of law during their terms of office and governed provinces afterwards, as did exconsuls.

Dental Stems (D,T)

ARIES, ARIETIS (m) ram; meaning in 25.5 unknown; Q reads ARBITROS.
COHORS, COHORTIS (f) company, troop, retinue; governor's staff.
COMES, COMITIS (m) companion.

Palatal Stems (C,G)

CALIX, CALICIS (m) wine cup; the Greek KYLIX.
LEX, LEGIS (f) law.

Nasal Stems (M,N): HOMO, HOMINIS (m) man, person.

Labial Stem (B,P): TRABS, TRABIS (f) beam, plank.

Person: PISO, PISONIS L. Calpurnius Piso, consul in 58 B.C. and governor of Macedonia from 57 to 55; Julius Caesar married his daughter; see appendix.

Fourth Declension

CASUS, CASUS (m) fall.
FLATUS, FLATUS (m) breath, blowing.
MANUS, MANUS (f) hand.
SITUS, SITUS (m) site, location.

Fifth Declension

PERNICIES, PERNICIEI (f) ruin, destruction.
RES, REI (f) thing, affair, situation.

GREEK NOUNS
FIRST DECLENSION MASCULINE

APHELIOTES, APHELIOTAE (m) Greek name for the east wind; nom -ES; gen -AE; dat -AE; acc -EN; abl -A; alt APELIOTES.
BOREAS, BOREAE (m) Boreas, the north wind; nom -AS; gen -AE; dat -AE; acc -AN; abl -A.
MIDAS, MIDAE (m) Midas, the famous king of Phrygia; declined like BOREAS.

ADJECTIVES
First-Second Declension

AMARUS bitter; comp AMARIOR, AMARIUS.
APTUS fit, suitable, appropriate.
ARANEOSUS full of spiders or spider webs.
AVITUS ancestral; cp AVUS (grandfather).
BELLUS pretty, fair; adv BELLE.
CINAEDUS loose, wanton, amoral.
DIVUS divine, deified.
EBRIOSUS drunk, inebriated; comp EBRIOSIOR, EBRIOSIUS.
EXPEDITUS free, light; perfect participle of EXPEDIO (liberate).
FALERNUS from the Falernian territory in Campania, famed for its wine; neuter used substantively = Falernian (wine).
IMULUS little lowest (part of), bottom (of); diminutive of IMUS (lowest).
INEPTUS inept, foolish.
LANEUS woolen, soft as wool.
LANGUIDUS weak, limp, languid.
LENTUS slow.
MAGNUS great.
MALUS bad, evil.
MERUS pure, often of wine that has not been diluted with water.
MEUS my, mine.
MINUTUS tiny, minute; perfect participle of MINUO (lessen).
MOLLICELLUS soft or gentle little; diminutive of MOLLIS.
MULTUS much; plural, many.
OPTIMUS best; superlative of BONUS.
SAETABUS of or from Saetabis, a Spanish town famous for fabrics.
SAEVUS savage, harsh.
SEVERUS severe, stern; comp SEVERIOR, SEVERIUS.
SUPINUS supine, lying back.
TURBIDUS wild, confused, chaotic.
TUUS your, yours.
THYNUS Bithynian.
VERUS true; adverb VERUM, VERE.
VETULUS little old; diminutive of VETUS.

RUS > ER: VESTER, VESTRA, VESTRUM your, yours.

Third Declension
I-Stems

HORRIBILIS, HORRIBILE horrible, frightening.
INANIS, INANE empty.
MOLLIS, MOLLE soft, gentle; comp MOLLIOR, MOLLIUS.
NOBILIS, NOBILE noble, eminent.
TURPIS, TURPE disgraceful, ugly; adverb TURPITER.

One Termination

INSOLENS (INSOLENTIS) unusual; immoderate, wild; adv INSOLENTER.
PAR (PARIS) equal.
PESTILENS (PESTILENTIS) unhealthy, destructive, pestilential.
RAPAX (RAPACIS) rapacious, greedy; comp RAPACIOR, RAPACIUS.

Irregular Comparative: MINOR, MINUS smaller, less; comp of PARVUS.

VERBS
First Conjugation

AESTUO, AESTUARE be agitated, boil, burn (AESTUES).
AMO, AMARE love (AMARI).
CONSCRIBILLO, CONSCRIBILLARE scribble on, mark (CONSCRIBILLENT).
DO, DARE, DEDI, DATUM give (DENT, DATUM, DEDISSES).
ELEVO, ELEVARE lighten, lift up; excuse (ELEVA).
INVOLO, INVOLARE fly upon (INVOLAVISTI > INVOLASTI).
IRRUMO, IRRUMARE force one's way in; obscene term referring to oral sex (IRRUMAVISTI > IRRUMASTI).
MIGRO, MIGRARE depart, leave, migrate (MIGRATE).
OSCITO, OSCITARE open the mouth, gape, yawn (OSCITANTES).
REGLUTINO, REGLUTINARE unglue, unstick, loosen (REGLUTINA).

Second Conjugation

HABEO, HABERE, HABUI, HABITUM have (HABET, HABERE).
JUBEO, JUBERE, JUSSI, JUSSUM order, command (JUBET).
LUBET, LUBERE impersonal verb, it is pleasing; alt LIBET.
PATEO, PATERE, PATUI lie or be open (PATET).
SOLEO, SOLERE, SOLITUS be accustomed or wont to do (SOLES).
VIDEO, VIDERE, VIDI, VISUM see; passive, seem.

Third Conjugation

DEPRENDO, DEPRENDERE, DEPRENDI, DEPRENSUM seize (DEPRENSA).
FERO, FERRE, TULI, LATUM carry, bear (TULISTIS).
GERO, GERERE, GESSI, GESTUM carry; carry on, do (GERITIS).
INGERO, INGERERE, INGESSI, INGESTUM carry in, deliver (INGER).
INURO, INUERE, INUSSI, INUSTUM burn in, brand, inflict (INUSTA).
OPPONO, OPPONERE, OPPOSUI, OPPOSITUM place against, expose to

(OPPOSITA EST).
OSTENDO, OSTENDERE, OSTENDI, OSTENSUM show, exhibit, display (OSTENDIT).
PETO, PETERE, PETII, PETITUM seek (PETE).
REFERO, REFERRE, RETULI, RELATUM bring back.
REMITTO, REMITTERE, REMISI, REMISSUM return, give back (REMITTE).
SEQUOR, SEQUI, SECUTUS follow.
SINO, SINERE, SIVI, SITUM allow, permit, leave alone (SINERES).

Third Conjugation IO: ABICIO, ABICERE, ABJECI, ABJECTUM throw away, dismiss (ABICE).

Fourth Conjugation

FARCIO, FACIRE, FARSI, FARTUM fill full, stuff (FARTI ESTIS).
VESANIO, VESANIRE be insane, rage (VESANIENTE).

Irregular Verbs

ABEO, ABIRE, ABII go away (ABITE).
INQUAM say; used for direct quotations (INQUIES).
MALO, MALLE, MALUI prefer; MAIUS (more) + UOLO (wish) (MALLEM).
SUM, ESSE, FUI be (ES, FUISTIS, FUERUNT, ESTIS, ERUNT, EST).

APPENDIX

During the consulship of L. Piso in 58, a bill was passed exiling Cicero for the execution of the Catilinarian conspirators. When Cicero returned to Rome he took advantage of several occasions to denounce Piso's career and especially his stewardship of Macedonia in 57, the same service denounced by Catullus in poem 28. Here is a passage typical of Cicero's abuse, from his speech DE PROVINCIIS CONSULARIBUS 3.5-6 ("Concerning the Allocation of Consular Provinces"): "In the past our armies subdued the neighboring tribes and crushed the barbarians. Macedonia was a land at peace. We guarded it with a small garrison commanded by subordinate officers. Rome's reputation alone was sufficient security. Now we have a former consul there with absolute authority over an entire army and the land is suffering so much that not even permanent peace could restore its prosperity. Meanwhile you all know that the Greeks are being forced to pay Piso a huge sum of money every year to support his military activities and that he has taken over the tax revenues and customs fees from the port of Dyrrachium and all but laid siege to our faithful ally Byzantium. When he was finally convinced that he could not extort any more money by force from the poor people of that town, he stationed his retinue there for the winter. He placed in charge the men he considered the most energetic criminal accomplices and the best ministers of his own lusts. But I will not describe his flagrantly illegal court decisions in this free city or mention the murders he sanctioned or his sexual assaults, for which there is one particularly galling piece of evidence that shall live forever in the annals of depravity and almost justifies the resentment that some people feel against our rule. I am referring to the established fact that a number of noble maidens threw themselves into wells and so escaped compulsory defilement with voluntary death. I am not passing over these charges because I consider them trivial but because I do not have a witness for them at present."

NOUNS
First Declension

ANIMA breath of life, soul.
BRITANNIA Britain.
CAELICOLA (mf) heaven dweller; deity.
GALLIA Gaul, modern France.
INSULA island.
MENTULA penis; diminutive of MENTUM (chin, beard).
NEBULA cloud.
PRAEDA booty, plunder.

Masculine Proper Name: MAMURRA a Roman EQUES or "knight" from Formiae; he became wealthy while serving under Caesar in Gaul as the commander of his engineers. His ostentatious spending and friendship with Caesar incurred Catullus' hostility. He refers to him as DECOCTOR FORMIANUS ("the bankrupt from Formiae") in poems 41 and 43 and as MENTULA in 94, 105, 114 and 115. We have evidence that Marmurra did not inspire affection even among his friends. Years after Catullus wrote, Cicero happened to be entertaining Caesar when word of Mamurra's death (circumstances unknown) was delivered. According to Cicero (ad Atticum 13.52.1), the dictator's facial expression did not change as he read the report.

Second Declension

AMICULUS little friend; diminutive of AMICUS.
COLUMBUS dove.
DEUS god (nom pl DI; gen pl DEORUM or DEUM; dat and abl plural DIIS or DIS).
TAGUS a river in Spain.
VENTUS wind.

Persons

ADONEUS Adonis, mythical Greek hunter, loved by Venus.
ALFENUS Alfenus Varus, a jurist and man of letters from Cremona.
ROMULUS legendary founder of Rome.

RUS > (E)R

GENER, GENERI son-in-law.
SOCER, SOCERI father-in-law.

Neuter

FACTUM deed, action; perfect participle of FACIO (make, do).
PATRIMONIUM inheritance, patrimony.

Third Declension

I-Stems

AMNIS, AMNIS (m) river.
CUBILE, CUBILIS (n) bed.
SODALIS, SODALIS (mf) comrade, companion.

N-Stems

ALEO, ALEONIS (m) gambler.
HOMO, HOMINIS (m) man, person.
NOMEN, NOMINIS (n) name; pretext or rationale for action, excuse.

R-Stems

AMOR, AMORIS (m) love.
IMPERATOR, IMPERATORIS (m) commander, general.

Dental Stems (D,T)

LIBERALITAS, LIBERALITATIS (f) liberality, generosity, nobility.
OCCIDENS, OCCIDENTIS (m) the "occident" or west (cp "orient"),
the region of the setting sun; present participle of OCCIDO,
OCCIDERE (fall, set).

Labial Stem (B,P): URBS, URBIS (f) city.

Fifth Declension: FIDES, FIDEI (f) trust.

Adjectives
First and Second Declension

AEREUS airy, windy; alt AERIUS.
ALBULUS little white; diminutive of ALBUS.
BONUS good.
CERTUS certain; adv CERTE.
CINAEDUS loose, wanton, amoral.
COMATUS hairy; GALLIA COMMATA = "forested Gaul" (France).
DIFFUTUTUS sexually exhausted; perfect participle of FUTUO.
DURUS hard; comp DURIOR, DURIUS.
FALSUS wrong; deceitful; perfect participle of FALLO (deceive).
HIBERUS Spanish.
IMPIUS impious, faithless, disloyal.
IMPUDICUS shameless.
INIQUUS unfair, unequal; adv INIQUE.
IRRITUS useless, vain.
MALUS bad, evil; adv MALE.
PATERNUS paternal.
PERFIDUS perfidious, treacherous; vocative PERFIDE.

PIUS pious, loyal; superlative PIISSIMUS.
PONTICUS Pontic, of or related to Pontus, the Black Sea.
PRIMUS first.
SECUNDUS second.
SUPERBUS proud.
TERTIUS third.
TUTUS safe; perfect participle of TUEOR (protect).
TUUS your, yours.
ULTIMUS farthest, most remote.
UNANIMUS of one spirit, harmonious.
UNICUS unique, only.
UNCTUS sleek, rich; comp UNCTIOR, UNCTIUS; perfect participle of
UNGO (anoint).

RUS > (E)R

AURIFER, AURIFERA, AURIFERUM gold-bearing or producing.
MISER, MISERA, MISERUM miserable.
SINISTER, SINISTRA, SINISTRUM left, on the left side;
unfavorable.

Third Declension Adjectives

I-Stems

DULCIS, DULCE sweet.
OMNIS, OMNE all, every.

One-Termination

FALLAX (FALLACIS) deceptive, treacherous.
IMMEMOR (IMMEMORIS) not remembering, forgetful.
OPULENS (OPULENTIS) rich, wealthy; superl voc OPULENTISSIME.
SUPERFLUENS (SUPERFLUENTIS) flowing over.
VORAX (VORACIS) voracious, greedy; comp VORACIOR, VORACIUS.

Verbs

1st Conjugation

DEVORO, DEVORARE devour.
DUBITO, DUBITARE hesitate (DUBITAS).
ELLUOR, ELLUARI, ELLUATUS feast, gourmandize (ELLUATUS EST).
EXPATRO, EXPATRARE spend an inheritance, patrimony (EXPATRAVIT).
LANCINO, LANCINARE rip apart, tear, rend (LANCINATA).
PERAMBULO, PERAMBULARE walk through (PERAMBULABIT).

2nd Conjugation

FOVEO, FOVERE, FOVI, FOTUM favor, foster (FOVETIS).
HABEO, HABERE, HABUI, HABITUM have (HABEBAT, HABEANT).

IUBEO, IUBERE, IUSSI, IUSSUM order, command (JUBEBAS).
MISEREO, MISERERE, MISERUI pity; impersonal MISERET ME ALICUIUS = pity for someone (genitive) affects me (accusative).
PAENITET, PAENITERE, PAENITUIT regret; impersonal PAENITET ME ALICUIUS = regret for something (genitive) affects me (accusative).
PLACEO, PLACERE, PLACUI please (PLACENT).
TIMEO, TIMERE, TIMUI fear (TIMETUR).
VIDEO, VIDERE, VIDI, VISUM, see; passive, seem (VIDEBIS).

3rd Conjugation

COMEDO, COMESSE, COMEDI, COMESUM eat up, devour (COMESSET).
DESERO, DESERERE, DESERUI, DESERTUM desert, forsake (DESERIS).
DICO, DICERE, DIXI, DICTUM say (DIC, DICTA).
FALLO, FALLERE, FALSI, FALSUM deceive, trick.
FERO, FERRE, TULI, LATUM carry, bear (FERES).
INDUCO, INDUCERE, INDUXI, INDUCTUM induce, lead into (INDUCENS).
NEGLEGO, NEGLEGERE, NEGLEXI, NEGLECTUM neglect (NEGLEGIS).
OBLIVISCOR, OBLIVISCI, OBLITUS forget (OBLITUS ES).
PERDO, PERDERE, PERDIDI, PERDITUM destroy, ruin (PERDIDISTIS).
PRODO, PRODERE, PRODIDI, PRODITUM put forth; expose, betray.
RETRAHO, RETRAHERE, RETRAXI, RETRACTUM pull back (RETRAHIS).
SINO, SINERE, SIVI, SITUM allow, permit, leave alone (SINIS).
TRADO, TRADERE, TRADIDI, TRADITUM hand over, give up.
UNGO, UNGERE, UNXI, UNCTUM anoint with oil (UNCTA).

Third Conjugation IO

FACIO, FACERE, FECI, FACTUM make, do (FACIET, FACIANT, FACTI, FACTA).
PATIOR, PATI, PASSUS endure, experience.

Fourth Conjugation: SCIO, SCIRE, SCIVI, SCITUM know (SCIT).

Irregular Verbs

MEMINI, MEMINISSE perfect forms with present meanings, remember (MEMINIT, MEMINERUNT).
POSSUM, POSSE, POTUI be able (POTEST).
SUM, ESSE, FUI be (ES, EST, SUNT, FORENT, FUISTI).

SEGMENT 12 (Poems 31-33)

NOUNS
First Declension

CURA care, concern.
DELICIAE delight, sweetheart; plural forms only.
INSULA island.
ORA shore, region.
RAPINA theft, robbery, pillaging.
TABELLA little board, tablet; door-sill.
THYNIA Bithynia, the province in northwestern Turkey.
TUNICA tunic.
UNDA wave.
VENIA grace, favor.

Person: IPSITHILLA one of Catullus' close friends.

SECOND DECLENSION
Masculine

CACHINNUS laughter, a laugh.
CAMPUS field.
CULUS ass, buttocks.
ERUS master.
FILIUS son.
LECTUS bed, couch.
OCELLUS little eye; diminutive of OCULUS; used figuratively like
English "jewel" for the best example of a class.
POPULUS people.

Persons

NEPTUNUS Neptune, god of the sea.
VIBENNIUS an unknown man abused in poem 33.

NEUTER

EXILIUM exile; alt EXSILIUM.
PALLIUM cloak, mantle.
STAGNUM a body of water, especially still water.

Third Declension
Liquid Stems (L,R)

FUR, FURIS (mf) thief.
LABOR, LABORIS (m) work, labor.
LAR, LARIS (m) guardian deity of a household or neighborhood.
LEPOR, LEPORIS (m) charm; plural as a term of endearment "my
enchantment."
PATER, PATRIS (m) father.

65

I-Stems

FORIS, IS (f) door; adverbs FORAS and FORIS outdoors, outside (originally an accusative of direction and an ablative of separation, respectively, based on the obsolete nominative singular FORA).
MARE, MARIS (n) sea.
NATES, NATIUM (f) buttocks; plural forms only.

N-STEMS

FUTUTIO, FUTUTIONIS (f) sexual intercourse.
LIMEN, LIMINIS (n) doorsill, threshhold.
SIRMIO, SIRMIONIS (f) a peninsula in Lake Garda near Verona.

S-Stems

AS, ASSIS (m) an as, a small copper coin, a penny.
ONUS, ONERIS (n) load, burden.

Dental Stem (D,T): MENS, MENTIS (f) mind.

Fourth Declension

DOMUS, DOMUS (f) house, home; locative DOMI at home.
LACUS, LACUS (m) lake.

ADJECTIVES
First-Second Declension

BALNEARIUS having to do with bath houses.
BEATUS blessed, fortunate; perfect participle of BEO (bless); comp BEATIOR, BEATIUS.
BITHYNUS Bithynian.
CINAEDUS loose, wanton, amoral.
CONTINUUS continuous, uninterrupted.
FESSUS weary, exhausted; perfect participle of FATISCOR (grow tired).
INQUINATUS defiled, dirty; comp INQUINATIOR, INQUINATIUS.
LAETUS happy.
LYDIUS of or from Lydia, the Etruscans' supposed homeland; hence Lydian = Etrurian = northern Italian.
MALUS bad, evil; adverb MALE.
MEUS my, mine.
OPTIMUS best; superlative of BONUS.
PEREGRINUS foreign.
PILOSUS hairy; cp PILUS (hair).
SUPINUS supine, lying on one's back.
TUTUS safe, protected; perfect participle of TUEOR (protect).
VASTUS vast, huge and empty.

VENUSTUS charming, lovely.
VERUS true; adv VERUM, VERE.

RUS > (E)R

DEXTER, DEXTRA, DEXTRUM right, on the right hand.
NOSTER, NOSTRA, NOSTRUM our, ours.
SATUR, SATURA, SATURUM full, full of food, satisfied.

Third Declension

I-Stem: DULCIS, DULCE sweet.

One Termination

LIBENS (LIBENTIS) glad, willing; adv LIBENTER.
VORAX (VORACIS) voracious, greedy; comp VORACIOR, VORACIUS.

VERBS
First Conjugation

ADJUVO, ADJUVARE, ADJUVI, ADJUTUS give aid to, assist (ADJUVATO).
AMO, AMARE love; in requests AMABO = "please."
DESIDERO, DESIDERARE desire (DESIDERATO).
MERIDIO, MERIDIARE take a nap at noon, a siesta; MERIDIATUM =
accusative supine, translate "to take a nap."
OBSERO, OBSERARE close, bolt, lock (OBSERES).
PARO, PARARE prepare, acquire (PARES).
VENDITO, VENDITARE try to sell, hawk; frequentative of VENDO
sell.

Second Conjugation

GAUDEO, GAUDERE, GAVISUS rejoice, be glad (GAUDE, GAUDENTE
{GAUDETE in Merrill}).
JACEO, JACERE, JACUI lie, recline.
JUBEO, JUBERE, JUSSI, JUSSUM order, command (JUBE, JUSSERIS,
JUBETO).
LUBET, LUBERE impersonal verb, it is pleasing; alt LIBET
(LUBEAT).
LIQUEO, LIQUERE, LIQUI be clear, liquid (LIQUENTIBUS).
MANEO, MANERE, MANSI remain, stay (MANEAS).
PRANDEO, PRANDERE, PRANDI have breakfast; PRANSUS active, having
eaten, being full.
RIDEO, RIDERE, RISI laugh (RIDETE).
SALVEO, SALVERE be well/healthy; imperative SALVE as a greeting,
"Hail!"
VIDEO, VIDERE, VIDI, VISUM see; passive, seem.

Third Conjugation

ACQUIESCO, ACQUIESCERE, ACQUIEVI to grow quiet, rest; alt ADQUIESCO (ACQUIESCIMUS).
AGO, AGERE, EGI, ACTUM drive, do, make (AGES).
CREDO, CREDERE, CREDIDI, CREDITUM believe (CREDENS).
FERO, FERRE, TULI, LATUM carry, bear (FERT).
INVISO, INVISERE, INVISI, INVISUM look upon, behold.
LINQUO, LINQUERE, LIQUI, LICTUM leave, abandon (LIQUISSE).
NOSCO, NOSCERE, NOVI, NOTUM know (NOTAE SUNT).
PERTUNDO, PERTUNDERE, PERTUDI, PERTUSUM push through, bore through.
REPONO, REPONERE, REPOSUI, REPOSITUM place back (REPONIT).
SOLUO, SOLUERE, SOLUI, SOLUTUM loosen, release (SOLUTIS).

Fourth Conjugation: VENIO, VENIRE, VENI come (VENIMUS, VENIAM).

Irregular Verbs

ABEO, ABIRE, ABII go away.
EO, IRE, II go (ITIS).
POSSUM, POSSE, POTUI, be able (POTES).
SUM, ESSE, FUI be (EST, SUNT).

NOUNS
First Declension
Feminine

DEA goddess.
DOMINA mistress.
LUNA moon.
MEDULLA marrow of a bone or the innermost part of anything.
MUSA Muse, goddess of art, poetry.
OLIVA olive tree.
PUELLA girl.
SILVA forest.
VERONA Verona, Catullus' hometown.
VIA road, way.

Person: DIANA maiden goddess of hunting, the Greek Artemis.

Masculine

AGRICOLA farmer.
POETA poet.

SECOND DECLENSION
Masculine

AMICUS friend.
DINDYMUS a mountain in Phrygia overlooking Pessinus, where Cybele's chief temple was located.
PAPYRUS papyrus, scroll.

Persons

CAECILIUS a poet and friend of Catullus, otherwise unknown.
ROMULUS legendary founder of Rome.

RUS > (E)R: PUER, PUERI boy.

NEUTER

COLLUM neck.
COMUM Como, a town in Northern Italy; called NOVUM COMUM (New Como) after Julius Caesar enlarged it.
TECTUM roof; building; perfect participle of TEGO (cover).

Third Declension
Nasal Stems

COGITATIO, COGITATIONIS (f) thought, reflection.
ITER, ITINERIS (n) road, journey.

JUNO, JUNONIS (f) Juno.
LUMEN, LUMINIS (n) light, lamp.
NOMEN, NOMINIS (n) name.

I-Stems

AMNIS, AMNIS (m) river.
IGNIS, IGNIS (m) fire.
MOENIA, MOENIUM (n) walls (of a city); plural forms only.
SODALIS, SODALIS (mf) comrade, companion.

Liquid Stems (L,R)

AMOR, AMORIS (m) love.
JUPPITER, the form of Jupiter's name used in exclamations and as the nominative case; genitive, JOVIS; dative, JOVI etc.
MATER, MATRIS (f) mother.

Dental Stems (D,T)

GENS, GENTIS (f) people, tribe, nation.
MONS, MONTIS (m) mountain.

S-Stems

LITUS, LITORIS (n) shore.
TEMPUS, TEMPORIS (n) time.

Palatal Stem (C,G): FRUGES, FRUGUM (f) fruits of the earth, crops; plural forms only.

Labial Stem (B,P): OPS, OPIS (f) power, support.

Fourth Declension

CURSUS, CURSUS (m) course, running.
MANUS, MANUS (f) hand.
SALTUS, SALTUS (m) woodland.

Fifth Declension

FIDES, FIDEI (f) trust.
PROGENIES, PROGENIEI (f) family, offspring.

ADJECTIVES
First-Second Declension

ANNUUS annual, lasting a year.
ANTIQUUS ancient, old; adv ANTIQUE.
BONUS good.
CANDIDUS bright, white.

DELIUS Delian, of or from Delos, Apollo's birthplace.
DOCTUS learned, educated; perfect participle of DOCEO (teach); comp DOCTIOR, DOCTIUS.
LARIUS Larian, of Larius, a lake in northern Italy.
LATONIUS of Latona, the mother of Apollo and Diana; Greek Leto.
LUCINUS bringing into light; JUNO LUCINA denotes Juno as a goddess of childbirth with whom Diana was also identified.
MAGNUS great.
MAXIMUS greatest, most; superlative of MAGNUS; adv MAXIME.
MENSTRUUS monthly.
MEUS my, mine.
MISELLUS poor little; diminutive of MISER (miserable).
NOTHUS illegitimate, not genuine.
NOVUS new.
PUERPERUS pregnant, childbearing.
RECONDITUS hidden, secret; perfect participle of RECONDO (put away).
RUSTICUS rustic.
SANCTUS holy, sacred; perfect participle of SANCIO (make sacred, consecrate).
SAPPHICUS of or associated with Sappho, the famous Greek poetess of Lesbos.
SUUS his, her, its or their own.
TRIVIUS of or associated with crossroads or intersections; Diana and Hecate may be called Trivia because their temples were frequently built at crossroads.
VENUSTUS charming, lovely; adv VENUSTE.
VERUS true; adv VERUM, VERE; comp VERIOR, VERIUS.

RUS > (E)R

INTEGER, INTEGRA, INTEGRUM whole; pure, uncorrupted.
TENER, TENERA, TENERUM tender, delicate.

Third Declension
One Termination

IMPOTENS (IMPOTENTIS) uncontrollable, raging; "powerless" only in the sense of being unable to exercise restraint.
POTENS (POTENTIS) powerful.
SOSPES (SOSPITIS) safe, unharmed.

Irregular comparative: INTERIOR, INTERIUS inner, interior.

VERBS
First Conjugation

INCOHO, INCOHARE begin (INCOHATA EST, INCOHATAM).
MOROR, MORARI, MORATUS delay, linger, wait.
NUNTIO, NUNTIARE announce (NUNTIANTUR).
REVOCO, REVOCARE call back (REVOCET).

71

ROGO, ROGARE ask, ask for something (ROGET).
SONO, SONARE make a noise, resound (SONANTUM).
SOSPITO, SOSPITARE preserve, protect (SOSPITES).
VORO, VORARE devour (VORABIT).

Second Conjugation

DOLEO, DOLERE, DOLUI suffer, feel sorry, grieve (DOLENTIBUS).
EXPLEO, EXPLERE, EXPLEVI, EXPLETUM fill up (EXPLES).
PLACEO, PLACERE, PLACUI please (PLACET).
SOLEO, SOLERE, SOLITUS semi-deponent, be accustomed to or wont to do (SOLITA ES).
VIREO, VIRERE, VIRUI be green, bloom (VIRENTIUM).

Third Conjugation

CANO, CANERE, CECINI, CANTUM sing (CANAMUS).
DEPONO, DEPONERE, DEPOSUI or DEPOSIVI, DEPOSITUM set or lay down (DEPOSIVIT).
DICO, DICERE, DIXI, DICTUM say, speak, tell (DICAS, DICTA ES).
EDO, EDERE, EDIDI, EDITUM give forth, put out, emit (EDUNT).
IGNOSCO, IGNOSCERE, IGNOVI, IGNOTUM ignore; with dative, to forgive someone for something.
LEGO, LEGERE, LEGI, LECTUM collect, gather; gather words, hence read -- its principal meaning in Catullus (LEGIT).
RECONDO, RECONDERE, RECONDIDI, RECONDITUM put away, store or hide (RECONDITORUM).
RELINQUO, RELINQUERE, RELIQUI, RELICTUM leave behind, abandon, desert (RELINQUENS).
TEGO, TEGERE, TEXI, TECTUM cover (TECTA).

Third Conjugation I-Forms

ACCIPIO, ACCIPERE, ACCEPI, ACCEPTUM receive, accept (ACCIPIAT).
INICIO, INICERE, INJECI, INJECTUM throw in or upon (INICIENS).

Fourth Conjugation

METIOR, METIRI, MENSUS measure, distribute, deal out (METIENS).
SAPIO, SAPIRE to have taste, to be wise or sensible (SAPIET).
VENIO, VENIRE, VENI come (VENIAT).

Irregular Verbs

DEPEREO, DEPERIRE, DEPERII perish, die; transitively, die for, love passionately (DEPERIT).
EO, IRE, II go (EUNTEM).
SUM, ESSE, FUI be (ES, EST, SUMUS, SIS, FORES).
VOLO, VELLE, VOLUI wish, be willing, desire (VELIM).

NOUNS
First Declension
Feminine

BARBA beard.
CARTA scroll, page; alt CHARTA.
INFACETIAE   vulgarity,   tastelessness;   plural   forms   only;   alt
INFICITIAE.
MENTULA penis; diminutive of MENTUM (chin, beard).
PILA pillar.
PUELLA girl.
TABERNA tavern, inn.
URINA urine.

Masculine: POETA poet.

SECOND DECLENSION
Masculine

DEUS god.
FILIUS son.
HIRCUS goat.
IAMBUS iamb, a poetic foot.
MOECHUS adulterer.
PONTUS sea.

Persons

EGNATIUS an emigrant from Spain who evidently achieved some
prominence   in Catullus' circle; he may have been the author of an
Epicurean   poem entitled DE RERUM NATURA -- like Lucretius'; he is
mentioned in poems 37 and 39.
VOLUSIUS   a   poet   ridiculed   by   Catullus   in   poem 36; he had
evidently composed an annalistic or year-by-year history of Rome
in verse, which Catullus nominates as the worst poem ever
written.

Neuter

LIGNUM wood, piece of wood, tablet.
VOTUM vow; perfect participle of VOVEO.

Third Declension
Dental Stems (D,T)

DENS, DENTIS (m) tooth.
FRONS, FRONTIS (f) forehead, brow, face; front.

N-Stems

CUPIDO, CUPIDINIS (m) Cupid.
SOPIO, SOPIONIS (f) apparently a colloquial word for penis.

I-Stems

ANNALES, ANNALIUM (m) yearly records, annals.
CONTUBERNALIS, CONTUBERNALIS (mf) tentmate, comrade; from CONTUBERNIUM (soldiers' tent).
IGNIS, IGNIS (m) fire.

S-Stems

RUS, RURIS (n) field, the countryside.
VENUS, VENERIS (f) Venus, the goddess of love.

Liquid Stems (L,R)

FRATER, FRATIS (m) brother.
SESSOR, SESSORIS (m) sitter.

Fourth Declension: SINUS, SINUS (m) lap, bosom; bay, gulf.

Place-names

CELTIBERIA Spain, central Spain.
HADRIA the Adriatic Sea.

CNIDUS town in southern Turkey famous for a temple of Venus.

GOLGI, GOLGORUM a town in Cyprus with a temple of Venus.
URII, URIORUM a town in southern Italy with a temple of Venus.

DURRACHIUM a city, known in earlier Greek history as Epidamnus, in modern Yugoslavia; the first stop on the sea journey from southern Italy to Greece.
IDALIUM town on Cyprus with temple of Venus.

AMATHUS, AMATHUNTIS (f) a town in southern Cyrpus; Greek accusative AMATHUNTA.
ANCON, ANCONIS (f) a town on the eastern coast of Italy, south of Venice and Ravenna; its name means headland -- from the Greek, ANCON, angle; Greek accusative ANCONA.

ADJECTIVES
First-Second Declension

APERTUS open, spacious; perfect participle of APERIO.
BEATUS blessed, fortunate; perfect participle of BEO (bless);

comp BEATIOR, BEATIUS.
BELLUS pretty, fair; adv BELLE.
BONUS good.
CAERULEUS blue.
CAPILLATUS long-haired.
CETERUS other; singular forms rare.
CONTINUUS   continuous,   uninterrupted;   adv   CONTINENTER
continuously, in a row.
CUNICULOSUS full of rabbits.
DIVUS divine, deified.
ELECTUS choice, special; superlative ELECTISSIMUS choicest, best;
perfect participle of ELIGO (pick out).
HARUNDINOSUS full of reeds.
HIBERUS Spanish.
ILLEPIDUS not charming, rude, boorish; alt INLEPIDUS.
INDIGNUS unworthy.
INSULSUS   unsalted;   insipid,   stupid,   tasteless,   awkward;
superlative INSULSISSIMUS.
INVENUSTUS lacking charm, boorish.
JOCOSUS full of jokes, funny, enjoyable; adv JOCOSE.
LEPIDUS charming, elegant; adv LEPIDE.
MAGNUS great.
MEUS my, mine.
NONUS ninth.
OPACUS dark.
PESSIMUS worst; superlative of MALUS.
PILLEATUS wearing a PILLEUS, a skull cap worn after gaining
freedom from slavery; also worn by Castor and Pollux.
PLENUS full, full of (with genitive).
PUSILLUS very small.
SANCTUS holy, sacred; perfect participle of SANCIO (dedicate).
SEMITARIUS associated with back alleys; vulgar; from SEMITA
(path).

Third Declension

I-Stem: OMNIS, OMNE all, every.

One Termination

INFELIX (INFELICIS) unproductive, sterile.
SALAX (SALACIS) lively, lusty.
TARDIPES (TARDIPEDIS) slow-footed.
TRUX (TRUCIS) rough, savage.

VERBS
First Conjugation

AMO, AMARE love (AMATIS, AMABITUR, AMATA).
CACO, CACARE "relieve oneself"; transitive, smear with excrement
(CACATA).

CREO, CREARE created (CREATA).
DEFRICO, DEFRICARE rub, polish (DEFRICATUS).
DO, DARE, DEDI, DATUM, give (DATURAM).
IRRUMO, IRRUMARE force one's way in; obscene term referring to oral sex.
PUGNO, PUGNARE fight (PUGNATA).
PUTO, PUTARE think (PUTATIS, PUTATE).
USTILO, USTILARE burn (USTILANDA).
VIBRO, VIBRARE brandish, shake menancingly.

Second Conjugation

AUDEO, AUDERE, AUSUS dare (AUSURUM).
LICET, LICERE, LICUIT impersonal verb with complementary infinitive; it is permissible (to do something).
SEDEO, SEDERE, SEDI sit (SEDETIS).
VIDEO, VIDERE, VIDI, VISUM see; passive, seem (VIDIT).
VOVEO, VOVERE, VOVI, VOTUM vow, promise something to the gods in exchange for a specific favor (VOVIT).

Third Conjugation

COLO, COLERE, COLUI, CULTUM take care of, cultivate a place, hence inhabit, dwell in.
CONFUTUO, CONFUTUERE, CONFUTUI, CONFUTUTUM take (sexually), debauch.
CONSIDO, CONSIDERE, CONSEDI sit together, take a seat in an assembly.
DESINO, DESINERE, DESII stop or cease (DESIISSEM > DESISSEM).
REDDO, REDDERE, REDDIDI, REDDITUM give back, return; of a vow, fulfill.
RESTITUO, RESTITUERE, RESTITUI, RESTITUTUM replace, restore, revive (RESTITUTUS ESSEM).
SCRIBO, SCRIBERE, SCRIPSI, SCRIPTUM write (SCRIBAM, SCRIPTA).
SINO, SINERE, SIVI, SITUM allow, permit, leave alone.
SOLVO, SOLVERE, SOLVI, SOLUTUM loosen, release.

Third Conjugation IO

ACCIPIO, ACCIPERE, ACCEPI, ACCEPTUM receive, accept.
FACIO, FACERE, FECI, FACTUM do make (FACE, FACIT).
FUGIO, FUGERE, FUGI flee, retreat (FUGIT).

Fourth Conjugation: VENIO, VENIRE, VENI come (VENITE).

Irregular Verbs: SUM, ESSE, FUI be (EST, SUNT, ESSEM).

NOUNS
First Declension
Feminine

CELTIBERIA Spain, central Spain.
GINGIVA gum.
HORA hour; IN HORAS every hour, hourly.
LACRIMA tear.
POENA punishment, penalty.
RIXA quarrel, brawl.
TERRA earth.

SECOND DECLENSION
Masculine

DEUS god.
FILIUS son.
IAMBUS iamb, a poetic foot.
MORBUS sickness, disease.
REUS the defendant in a legal dispute.
ROGUS funeral pyre.
VENTUS wind.

Neuter with masculine endings: VULGUS the masses, the mob.

Persons

CATULLUS the author.
CORNIFICIUS the thoughtless friend of poem 38, possibly Quintus Cornificius, a poet and politician whose death many years later could be attributed to his insensitivity. During the civil war that followed Caesar's assasination, he fell into conflict with his erstwhile allies Ocatavian and Antony and was killed by their troops when his own deserted him because (according to St. Jerome) he had begun referring to them in jest as GALEATI LEPORES ("armed bunnies").
EGNATIUS the Spaniard in Catullus' circle; see segment 14.
RAVIDUS the cognomen, meaning dark, of an unknown person.

NEUTER

LOTIUM urine; genitive LOTI.
SUBSELLIUM bench.

Third Declension
Dental Stems (D,T)

DENS, DENTIS (m) tooth.
MENS, MENTIS (f) mind.

Liquid Stems (L,R)

AMOR, AMORIS (m) love.
MATER, MATRIS (f) mother.
ORATOR, ORATORIS (m) orator, speaker.

S-Stem; OS, ORIS (mouth, face).

Nasal Stem (N): ADLOCUTIO, ADLOCUTIONIS (f) salutation, greeting; alt ALLOCUTIO.

I-Stem: MANE morning; indeclinable neuter; also used adverbially - "in the morning"

Fourth Declension

FLETUS, FLETUS (m) weeping, mourning.
RISUS, RISUS (m) laughter, a laugh.

Fifth Declension

DIES, DIEI (mf) day; IN DIES every day, daily.
RES, REI (f) thing, affair, situation.

ADJECTIVES
First-Second Declension

AMPLUS large, ample, abundant; comp AMPLIOR, AMPLIUS.
BONUS good.
CANDIDUS bright, white.
DENTATUS toothy.
ETRUSCUS Etruscan, the ancient people of northern Italy.
EXPOLITUS polished; perfect participle of EXPOLIO; comp EXPOLITIOR, EXPOLITIUS.
INEPTUS foolish, stupid; adv INEPTE; comp INEPTIOR, INEPTIUS.
LABORIOSUS laborious; adv LABORIOSE.
LANUVINUS Lanuvian, from Lanuvium, a town near Rome.
LONGUS long, far; long-lived.
MAESTUS sad, grieving; comp MAESTIOR, MAESTIUS.
MALUS bad, evil; adv MALE; MALEST = MALE EST.
MEUS my, mine.
MINIMUS very small, smallest; superlative of PARVUS.
MISELLUS poor little; diminutive of MISER (miserable).
OBESUS obese, fat; perfect participle of OBEDO (devour).
ORBUS bereft, widowed, alone.
PARCUS thrifty, frugal; lean, small.
PAULUS little, small.
PURUS pure, clean; adv PURITER.
RUSSUS red.
SABINUS Sabine, an ancient Italian people.

SIMONIDEUS Simonidean, of or like Simonides, an early Greek poet famed for the melancholy beauty of his verse.
TRANSPADANUS Transpadane, of or associated with Italy north of the Po, the area where Catullus' hometown, Verona, is located.
TUUS your, yours.
UNICUS unique, only.
URBANUS urbane; of or from the city.

RUS > (E)R

ATER, ATRA, ATRUM dark, black.
CELTIBER, CELTIBERA, CELTIBERUM Celtiberian; Spanish, designating inhabitants of central Spain.
UMBER, UMBRA, UMBRUM Umbrian, member of that tribe of Italians.
VESTER, VESTRA, VESTRUM your, yours.

Third Declension

I-Stems: FACILIS, FACILE easy; superlative FACILLIMUS.

One Termination

ELEGANS (ELEGANTIS) elegant.
PRAECEPS (PRAECIPITIS) headfirst, headlong.
TIBURS (TIBURTIS) Tiburtan, of or associated with Tibur, a town in Latium, now Tivoli.
VECORS (VECORDIS) mad, insane.

VERBS
First Conjugation

ADVOCO, ADVOCARE call, summon, addressed (ADVOCATUS).
AMO, AMARE love.
ARBITROR, ARBITRARI, ARBITRATUS judge, think.
DEFRICO, DEFRICARE rub, polish.
EXCITO, EXCITARE excite, arouse (EXCITAT).
OPTO, OPTARE wish, desire (OPTAS).
PARO, PARARE prepare, obtain (PARAT).
PRAEDICO, PRAEDICARE proclaim, announce (PRAEDICET).
SOLOR, SOLARI, SOLATUS comfort, console (SOLATUS ES).

Second Conjugation

FLEO, FLERE, FLEVI weep, mourn (FLET).
HABEO, HABERE, HABUI, HABITUM have (HABET).
LUGEO, LUGERE, LUXI weep, mourn (LUGETUR impersonal passive).
MONEO, MONERE, MONUI, MONITUM warn, advise (MONENDUM EST).
RENIDEO, RENIDERE, RENIDUI smile again or repeatedly; literally, shine again (RENIDET).
SOLEO, SOLERE, SOLITUS semi-deponent, be accustomed or wont to do (SOLET).

Third Conjugation

AGO, AGERE, EGI, ACTUM drive, do (AGIT).
ATTINGO, ATTINGERE, ATTIGI, ATTACTUM touch (ATTINGAM).
BIBO, BIBERE, BIBI drink (BIBISSE).
IRASCOR, IRASCI, IRATUS become angry.
MINGO, MINGERE, MINXI urinate (MINXIT).
NOSCO, NOSCERE, NOVI, NOTUM know (NOTUS ESSE).

Fourth Conjugation

PERVENIO, PERVENIRE, PERVENI arrive, come to a place (PERVENIAS).
VENIO, VENIRE, VENI, VENTUM come, go (VENTUM EST impersonal passive).

Irregular Verbs

LAVO, LAVARE or LAVERE, LAVI, LAUTUM bathe, wash; both first and third conjugation forms occur; LAVIT in 39 respresents a third conjugation present.
NOLO, NOLLE, NOLUI be unwilling (NOLLEM).
SUM, ESSE, FUI be (ES, EST, ESSES, ERIS).
VOLO, VELLE, VOLUI want, wish, be willing (VIS, VOLUISTI)

NOUNS
First Declension
Feminine

AMICA girlfriend.
CURA care, concern.
LINGUA tongue.
MOECHA adulteress.
PROUINCIA province; division of the Roman empire.
PUELLA girl.

Persons

AMEANA Mamurra's mistress.
LESBIA Catullus' mistress.

SECOND DECLENSION
Masculine

AMICUS friend.
CATULUS young animal; puppy.
CODICILLI writing tablets; plural forms only.
DIGITUS finger.
HENDECASYLLABUS hendecasyllabic, a line of verse consisting of
eleven (Greek HENDEKA) syllables.
JOCUS joke.
MEDICUS physician, doctor.
MODUS method, manner.
NASUS nose.
OCELLUS little eye; diminutive of OCULUS.

NEUTER

LUTUM mud, filth.
SAECLUM age, generation.

Third Declension

Liquid Stems (L,R)

DECOCTOR, DECOCTORIS (m) bankrupt; literally one who has "boiled
away" (DECOXIT) his money.
LUPANAR, LUPANARIS (n) whorehouse, brothel; from LUPA (female
wolf), a slang term for prostitute.
RUBOR, RUBORIS (m) redness, blush.

S-Stems

AES, AERIS (n) copper, bronze.
AS, ASSIS (m) an as, a small coin, a penny.
OS, ORIS (n) mouth, face.

Palatal (C,G): VOX, VOCIS (f) voice.

Dental (D,T): PES, PEDIS (m) foot.

Nasal: RATIO, RATIONIS (f) reason; plan, rationale.

I-Stem: CANIS, CANIS (mf) dog.

ADJECTIVES
First-Second Declension

ALTUS high; comp ALTIOR, ALTIUS.
AMPLUS large; comp AMPLIOR, AMPLIUS.
BELLUS pretty, fair.
DEFUTUTUS sexually exhausted; from perfect participle of FUTUO.
FERREUS iron-like, metallic.
FORMIANUS of or from FORMIAE, a town in the vicinity of Rome.
GALLICANUS Gallic, French.
IMAGINOSUS full of images; from IMAGO, IMAGINIS (image).
INFACETUS lacking wit, unsophisticated, boorish.
LONGUS long.
MIMICUS like a mime, grotesque; adv MIMICE.
MINIMUS very small, smallest; superlative of PARVUS.
MOLESTUS annoying, irritating; adv MOLESTE.
PERDITUS destroyed, ruined; comp PERDITIOR, PERDITIUS; perfect participle of PERDO (destroy).
PROBUS good, proper.
PROPINQUUS near, neighboring; subst PROPINQUUS = neighbor.
PUDICUS modest, proper, chaste.
PUTIDUS rotten.
SANUS sane, healthy; adv SANE reasonably, truly, doubtlessly.
SICCUS dry.
TURPICULUS ugly little; diminutive of TURPIS, TURPE (ugly).

RUS > (E)R

NIGER, NIGRA, NIGRUM black, dark.
NOSTER, NOSTRA, NOSTRUM our, ours.
VESTER, VESTRA, VESTRUM your, yours.

Third Declension
I-Stems

OMNIS, OMNE all, every.
PUGILLARIS, PUGILLARE of the hand or fist; subst PUGILLARES, PUGILLARIUM handbooks; small writing tablets.
TURPIS, TURPE ugly; adv TURPE or TURPITER.

One Termination

ELEGANS (ELEGANTIS) elegant.
INSAPIENS (INSAPIENTIS) unwise, stupid.

VERBS
First Conjugation

COMPARO, COMPARARE compare, equate (COMPARATUR).
CONCLAMO, CONCLAMARE shout (together), raise a shout (CONCLAMATE).
CONVOCO, CONVOCARE call together, assemble (CONVOCATE).
MUTO, MUTARE to change (MUTANDA).
NARRO, NARRARE narrate, recount (NARRAT).
NEGO, NEGARE deny (NEGAT).
PUTO, PUTARE think (PUTAT, PUTANDUM).
REFLAGITO, REFLAGITARE demand again (REFLAGITEMUS, REFLAGITATE).
ROGO, ROGARE ask (ROGARE).

Second Conjugation

MOVEO, MOVERE, MOVI, MOTUM move (MOVETUR).
RIDEO, RIDERE, RISI laugh (RIDENTEM).
SALVEO, SALVERE be well/healthy; imperative, Hail! (SALVE).
SOLEO, SOLERE, SOLITUS be accustomed or wont to do (SOLET).
VIDEO, VIDERE, VIDI, VISUM see (VIDETIS).

Third Conjugation

CIRCUMSISTO, CIRCUMSISTERE, CIRCUMSTETI surround (CIRCUMSISTITE).
EXPRIMO, EXPRIMERE, EXPRESSI, EXPRESSUM force out, press out (EXPRIMAMUS).
INCEDO, INCEDERE, INCESSI walk, go (INCEDERE).
PERSEQUOR, PERSEQUI, PERSECUTUS follow after (PERSEQUAMUR).
POSCO, POSCERE, POPOSCI demand (POPOSCIT).
QUAERO, QUAERERE, QUAESIVI, QUAESITUM seek, ask (QUAERITIS).
REDDO, REDDERE, REDDIDI, REDDITUM give back (REDDITURAM, REDDE).

Third Conjugation IO

FACIO, FACERE, FECI, FACTUM do, make; consider, esteem (FACIS).
PATIOR, PATI, PASSUS endure, suffer, experience (PATI).
PROFICIO, PROFICERE, PROFECI, PROFECTUM make progress, profit (PROFICIMUS, PROFICERE).

Irregular Verbs

ADSUM, ADESSE, ADFUI be present (ADESTE).
POSSUM, POSSE, POTUI, be able (POTESTIS, POTEST, POTES).
SUM, ESSE, FUI be (ESSE, ESTIS, SIT, EST).

NOUNS
First Declension
Feminine

BRITTANIA Britain, England.
CENA dinner.
CONVIVA (mf) banqueter, guest.
DELICIAE delight, sweetheart.
INDIA India.
LIBYA Libya.
MEDULLA marrow; innermost part.
PESTILENTA pestilence, plague.
SYRIA Syria.
URTICA nettles (eaten by vegetarians).
VILLA villa, wealthy home in the countryside.
VITA life.

Greek First Declension: ACME high point; woman's name; acc ACMEN.

Second Declension
Masculine

ANIMUS soul, spirit.
ANNUS year.
DOMINUS lord, master.
FUNDUS ground; grounds, estate.
OCELLUS little eye; diminutive of OCULUS.

Persons

ANTIUS a man attacked in an oration by Sestius.
CATULLUS the author.
SEPTIMILLUS diminutive of Septimius.
SEPTIMIUS common first name; Acme's lover.
SESTIUS Publius Sestius, a politician who was famous for dull oratory and witless jokes. The humor of poem 44 depends on the fact that boring speeches were described as "frigid." According to Catullus, Sestius' denunciation of Antius was so frigid that he caught a cold from reading it and had to miss dinner at Sestius' house. Cicero made similiar jokes at Sestius' expense. For example, while abroad, he wrote to a friend in Rome (AD FAM. 7.32.1): AIS ENIM UT EGO DISCESSERIM, OMNIA OMNIUM DICTA -- IN HIS SESTIANA -- IN ME CONFERRI. QUID? TU ID PATERIS? NON DEFENDIS? ("You say that since I've been gone everybody's witty sayings are being attributed to me — including Sestius'. What? Do you permit that? Why don't you defend me?")

LIBER, LIBRI book.
PUER, PUERI boy.

Neuter

AUSPICIUM omen, sign, auspices.
GREMIUM bosom, lap.
OTIUM leisure, idleness.
VENENUM poison.

Third Declension
Nasal Stems (N)

ADPROBATIO, ADPROBATIONIS (f) approval, blessing.
GRAVEDO, GRAVEDINIS (f) a cold, headache; M's GRAVIDO at 44.12 is
a misprint.
HOMO, HOMINIS (m) man, person.
LEO, LEONIS (m) lion.
LIBIDO, LIBIDINIS (f) desire, passion.
ORATIO, ORATIONIS (f) speech, oration.

Dental Stems (D,T)

CAPUT, CAPITIS (n) head.
COR, CORDIS (n) heart; CORDI EST = it is pleasing.
GRATES (f) thanks; plural forms only.

Liquid Stems (L,R)

AMOR, AMORIS (m) love.
PETITOR, PETITORIS (m) seeker; plaintiff in a trial or candidate
in an election.
VENTER, VENTRIS (m) stomach, belly.

S-Stems

FRIGUS, FRIGORIS (n) cold.
OS, ORIS (n) mouth, face.
PECTUS, PECTORIS (n) breast, chest.
PIGNUS, PIGNORIS (n) token, proof.
VENUS, VENERIS (f) Venus, goddess of love.

I-Stems

IGNIS, IGNIS (m) fire.
TUSSIS, TUSSIS (f) cough; acc TUSSIM.

Fourth Declension: SINUS, SINUS (m) lap, bosom; bay.

ADJECTIVES
First-Second Declension

ASSIDUUS constant; adv ASSIDUE; alt ADSIDUUS.
AUSPICATUS fortunate, blessed, well-omened.
BEATUS blessed, fortune; perfect participle of BEO (bless); comp
BEATIOR, BEATIUS.
BONUS good.
CAESIUS blue, grey.
EBRIUS drunk.
FRIGIDUS cold, frigid.
MALUS bad, evil.
MAXIMUS most, greatest; superlative of MAGNUS.
MEUS my, mine.
MISELLUS poor little; diminutive of MISER (miserable).
MULTUS much, many.
MUTUUS mutual.
NEFARIUS evil, unholy, nefarious.
OBVIUS in the way, meeting; modified by dative.
PERDITUS ruined; adv ("ruinously, fatally") PERDITE; perfect
participle of PERDO (ruin).
PLENUS full, full of (with genitive).
PLURIMUS most; superlative of MULTUS; adv PLURIMUM.
PURPUREUS purple.
SABINUS Sabine.
SESTIANUS Sestian, belonging to Sestius.
SUMPTUOSUS sumptuous, expensive; full of SUMPTUS (expense).
SUUS his, her, its or their own.
TUUS your, yours.
VERUS true; adv VERUM, VERE; comp VERIOR, VERIUS.

RUS > (E)R

DEXTER, DEXTRA, DEXTRUM right, on the right hand.
NOSTER, NOSTRA, NOSTRUM our, ours.
SINISTER, SINISTRA, SINISTRUM left, on the left hand.

Third Declension
I-Stems

DULCIS, DULCE sweet.
FIDELIS, FIDELE faithful.
LEVIS, LEVE light; adv LEVITER.
MOLLIS, MOLLE soft, gentle.
OMNIS, OMNE all, every.
POTIS, POTE able, capable; POTE sometimes = POTEST.

One Termination

FREQUENS (FREQUENTIS) frequent, crowded.
INMERENS (INMERENTIS) undeserving; alt IMMERENS.

86

LIBENS (LIBENTIS) glad, willing; adv LIBENTER.
TIBURS (TIBURTIS) Tiburtan, of Tibur, a town in Italy.

Three Termination: ACER, ACRIS, ACRE sharp, bitter; comp ACRIOR, ACRIUS.

Irregular Comparative: MAIOR, MAIUS more.

VERBS
First Conjugation

AMO, AMARE love (AMANT, AMANTUR).
AUTUMO, AUTUMARE say, assert (AUTUMANT).
DEPRECOR, DEPRECARI, DEPRECATUS pray against, object, protest.
DO, DARE, DEDI, DATUM give (DEDIT).
PECCO, PECCARE err, sin; subst PECCATUM error.
QUASSO, QUASSARE shake around; frequentative of QUATIO (QUASSAVIT).
RECURO, RECURARE cure, restore (RECURAVI).
SUAVIOR, SUAVIARI, SUAVIATUS kiss; alt SAVIOR (SUAVIATA).
VOCO, VOCARE call (VOCAT).

Second Conjugation

ARDEO, ARDERE, ARSI burn, glow (ARDET).
TENEO, TENERE, TENUI, TENTUM hold, keep (TENENS).
TORREO, TORRERE, TORRUI, TOSTUM bake, burn, scorch (TOSTA).
VIDEO, VIDERE, VIDI, VISUM see (VIDIT).

Third Conjugation

AGO, AGERE, EGI, ACTUM drive, do; make; AGERE GRATES thank.
APPETO, APPETERE, APPETIVI, APPETITUM seek; alt ADPETO.
DICO, DICERE, DIXI, DICTUM say, tell (DIXIT).
EXPELLO, EXPELLERE, EXPULI, EXPULSUM cast out, expel.
FERO, FERRE, TULI, LATUM carry, bear (FERAT).
LAEDO, LAEDERE, LAESI, LAESUM wound, injure.
LEGO, LEGERE, LEGI, LECTUM gather; read.
PROFICISCOR, ,PROFICISCI, PROFECTUS set forth, depart (PROFECTI).
RECIPIO, RECIPERE, RECEPI, RECEPTUM get back, recover; archaic future perfect RECEPSO = RECEPERO.
REFLECTO, REFLECTERE, REFLEXI, REFLECTUM bend back (REFLECTENS).
SCRIBO, SCRIBERE, SCRIPSI, SCRIPTUM write (SCRIPTA).
STERNUO, STERNUERE, STERNUI sneeze (STERNUIT).
ULCISCOR, ULCISCI, ULTUS avenge, get even (at 44.17 Q's ES ULTU' = ES ULTUS; M has ES ULTA).

Third Conjugation IO

FACIO, FACERE, FECI, FACTUM make, do (FACIT).
FUGIO, FUGERE, FUGI flee.

REFICIO, REFICERE, REFECI, REFECTUM restore, repair.

Fourth Conjugation

SERVIO, SERVIRE, SERVII serve, be a servant to (SERVIAMUS).
VENIO, VENIRE, VENI come, go.

Irregular Verbs

INQUAM say (INQUIT)
MALO, MALLE, MALUI prefer, want more (MAVULT).
PEREO, PERIRE, PERII perish, be ruined; trans, love desperately.
SUM, ESSE, FUI be (ES, EST).
VOLO, VELLE, VOLUI wish, be willing, desire.

SEGMENT 18 (Poems 46-49)

NOUNS
First Declension
Feminine

ARISTA the beard on a stalk of grain; the stalk itself.
ASIA Asia; the Roman province of Asia corresponded roughly to modern Turkey.
AURA wind, air, breeze; Q preserves the archaic form AUREIS for AURIS.
GRATIA favor; plural, thanks.
NICAEA a city in Bithynia.
VIA road, way.

Masculine: POETA poet.

SECOND DECLENSION
Masculine

ANNUS year.
CAMPUS field.
MUNDUS the universe, the world.
OCULUS eye.
PATRONUS patron.
VERPUS a circumcised man, a term of abuse, used in apposition with Priapus in 47 to describe Piso.
ZEPHYRUS the west wind; the native Roman Favonius.

Persons

CATULLUS the author.
FABULLUS Veranius' companion in Spain and Macedonia; see segment 5.
IUVENTIUS the youth loved by Catullus; see segment 10.
MARCUS a common first name; see Tullius below.
PORCIUS a distinguished Roman family name, eg MARCUS PORCIUS CATO; the Porcius of poem 47 was evidently a member of Piso's infamous staff in Macedonia (see segment 10 appendix).
PRIAPUS a fertility god, son of Venus, distinguished by huge phallus.
ROMULUS legendary founder of Rome.
TULLIUS Marcus Tullius Cicero, the famous orator whose speeches and letters are the principal source of information about this period. One of his worst enemies was Clodius Pulcher, "Lesbia's" brother. It is not known what Catullus thanks Cicero for in poem 49.
VERANIOLUS little Veranius; diminutive of VERANIUS; see segment 4.

RUS > (E)R: AGER, AGRI field.

89

NEUTER

CAELUM sky.
CONVIVIUM feast, banquet.
STUDIUM zeal, enthusiasm.
TRIVIUM crossroads, intersection.

Greek Second Declension Neuter: SOCRATION little Socrates, Catullus' nickname for one of Piso's comrades.

Third Declension
Dental Stems (D,T)

COMES, COMITIS (mf) companion.
MENS, MENTIS (f) mind.
NEPOS, NEPOTIS (mf) grandchild, descendant.
PES, PEDIS (m) foot.
SEGES, SEGETIS (f) wheatfield.

Liquid Stems (L,R)

FUROR, FURORIS (m) madness.
TEPOR, TEPORIS (m) heat, warmth.
VER, VERIS (n) spring.

Nasal-Stems (N)

OSCULATIO, OSCULATIONIS (f) kissing.
VOCATIO, VOCATIONIS (f) summoning, invitation.

I-Stems

FAMES, FAMIS (f) hunger.
SODALIS, SODALIS (mf) comrade, companion.

Labial Stem (BP): URBS, URBIS (f) city.

Persons: PISO, PISONIS Lucius Calpurnius Piso, consul in 58 B.C. and the governor of Macedonia from 57 to 55; see segment 10.

Fourth Declension

COETUS, COETUS (m) assembly, group.
DOMUS, DOMUS (f) house, home; ablative of separation as if from 2nd declension A DOMO (from home).

Fifth Declension

DIES, DIEI (mf) day; DE DIE starting in the daytime, daylong.
SCABIES, SCABIEI (f) scabies, itchiness, mange.

ADJECTIVES
First-Second Declension

AESTUOSUS hot, boiling.
ARIDUS dry.
CLARUS famous.
DENSUS dense; comp DENSIOR, DENSIUS.
DISERTUS eloquent; superlative DISERTISSIMUS.
DIVERSUS diverse, turned or heading in different directions; perfect participle of DIVERTO (turn away).
EGELIDUS thawing, melting; cp. GELIDUS (cold, frosty).
IUCUNDUS pleasant, jocund.
LAETUS happy; comp LAETIOR, LAETIUS.
LAUTUS elegant, chic; perfect participle of LAVO (wash, bathe).
LONGUS long, far; adv LONGE.
MAXIMUS most, greatest.
MELLITUS honeyed.
MEUS my, mine.
OPTIMUS best; superlative of BONUS.
PESSIMUS worst; superlative of MALUS.
PHRYGIUS Phrygian; Phrygia was the ancient kingdom of central Turkey.
SUMPTUOSUS sumptuous, expensive; adv SUMPTUOSE.
TUUS your, yours.
VARIUS various, miscellaneous; adv VARIE.

RUS > (E)R

NOSTER, NOSTRA, NOSTRUM our, ours.
SATUR, SATURA, SATURUM full, full of food, satisfied.
SINISTER, SINISTRA, SINISTRUM left, on the left side; unfavorable; SINISTRA used substantively for "left hand."

Third Declension
I-Stems

AEQUINOCTIALIS, AEQUINOCTIALE equinoctial, at the beginning of spring.
DULCIS, DULCE sweet.
OMNIS, OMNE all, every.

One Termination: UBER (UBERIS) rich.

VERBS
First Conjugation

BASIO, BASIARE to kiss (BASIEM).
PRAETREPIDO, PRAETREPIDARE tremble, tremble beforehand, i.e. with anticipation (PRAETREPIDANS).
REPORTO, REPORTARE carry or bring back (REPORTANT).

VAGOR, VAGARI, VAGATUS wander, roam.
VOLO, VOLARE fly (VOLEMUS).

Second Conjugation

AVEO, AVERE desire, long, yearn (AVET).
VALEO, VALERE, VALUI be well or strong; as a substitute for POSSUM with a complementary infinitive, to be strong enough to do something; imperative VALE! = farewell (VALETE).
VIDEO, VIDERE, VIDI, VISUM see; passive, seem (VIDEAR).

Third Conjugation

AGO, AGERE, EGI, ACTUM drive, do, make; AGERE GRATES/GRATIAS to thank (AGIT).
LINQUO, LINQUERE, LIQUI, LICTUM leave, abandon (LINQUANTUR).
PRAEPONO, PRAEPONERE, PRAEPOSUI, PRAEPOSITUM to place someone (accusative) in front of or in charge of someone else (dative); set above, prefer (PRAEPOSUIT).
PROFICISCOR, PROFICISCI, PROFECTUS set forth, depart (PROFECTOS).
QUAERO, QUAERERE, QUAESIVI, QUAESITUM seek (QUAERUNT).
REFERO, REFERRE, RETULI, RELATUM bring back (REFERT).
SILESCO, SILESCERE fall silent, become still (SILESCIT).
SINO, SINERE, SIVI, SITUM allow, permit, leave alone (SINAT).
VIGESCO, VIGESCERE, VIGUI begin to be lively or vigorous; inceptive form of VIGEO be lively, flourish (VIGESCUNT).

Third Conjugation IO: FACIO, FACERE, FECI, FACTUM do, make (FACITIS).

Irregular Verbs: SUM, ESSE, FUI be (SUNT, FUERUNT > FUERE, ERUNT, SIT, FUTURUS)

NOUNS
First Declension
Feminine

DEA goddess.
FACETIAE wit; plural forms only.
FLAMMA flame.
LESBIA Catullus' mistress.
LINGUA tongue.
POENA punishment, penalty.
SELLA chair; SELLA CURULIS curule throne, an ornate chair reserved for higher magistrates.
STRUMA a scrofulous tumor, ie one on the neck from swollen lymph glands.
TABELLA little board, tablet; writing tablet.

SECOND DECLENSION
Masculine

CIBUS food.
DEUS god.
JOCUS joke.
LECTUS bed, couch.
NUMERUS number; rhythm, kind of verse.
SOMNUS sleep.

Diminutves

LECTULUS little bed, couch; cp LECTUS.
OCELLUS little eye; cp OCULUS.
VERSICULUS little verse; cp VERSUS.

Persons

CATULLUS the author.
LICINIUS Catullus' friend Gaius Licinius Calvus; see segment 6.
NONIUS a couple of minor politicians bearing this name are known to have supported Caesar.
VATINIUS Publius Vatinius, a loyal supporter of Caesar whose most noteworthy activity occurred in 59 BC when as a tribune he helped secure command of Gaul for Caesar. After his election to the praetorship in 55 BC, he was tried for bribery and acquitted with the help of Cicero on the defense. The prosecutor was Catullus' friend, Calvus, whose denunciation of Vatinius won him lasting fame as an orator. Poem 53 records the effect of his speech on one member of the audience. Supposedly even Vatinius was so impressed that he interrupted Calvus to ask whether it was fair for him to be convicted just because the prosecutor was so eloquent (Seneca CONTROVERSIAE VII.4,6). As this anecdote

suggests, Vatinius seems to have had an engaging, self-deprecating sense of humor, despite the bad press he gets from Catullus. He was also famous for making jokes about his own physical appearance, which was marred by tumors on his neck and varicose veins (Seneca DE CONSTANTIA SAPIENTIS 17). After election to the praetorship, the next step was the only higher office, the consulship. In poem 52, Vatinius is so certain that he will be elected to that too that he swears by it. In fact, Vatinius was never elected to the consulship. He remained loyal to Caesar, however, and after the end of the civil war with Pompey Caesar appointed him to serve as consul for the last couple of months of the year 47, for which no regular elections had been held. Vatinius' abbreviated consulship gave rise to one of Cicero's famous jests (Macrobius II.3.5): MAGNUM OSTENTUM ANNO VATINII FACTUM EST, QUOD ILLO CONSULE NEC BRUMA NEC VER NEC AESTAS NEC AUTUMNUS FUIT. ("A great portent occurred during Vatinius' year; when he was consul, there was no winter ... no spring, no summer, no fall.")

NEUTER

MEMBRUM joint, limb.
OTIUM leisure, idleness.
VINUM wine.

Third Declension
Dental Stems (D,T)

NOX, NOCTIS (f) night.
POEMA, POEMATIS (n) poem.
QUIES, QUIETIS (f) rest, quiet.

Liquid Stems (L,R)

DOLOR, DOLORIS (m) sorrow.
FUROR, FURORIS (m) madness.
LABOR, LABORIS (m) work, labor.
LEPOR, LEPORIS (m) charm.

Palatal Stems (C,G)

LUX, LUCIS (f) light.
PREX, PRECIS (f) prayer.
REX, REGIS (m) king.

I-Stems

AURIS, AURIS (f) ear.
NEMESIS, NEMESIS (f) revenge, retribution; often personified.

Labial Stem: URBS, URBIS (f) city.

94

Nasal Stem: LUMEN, LUMINIS (n) light.

Indeclinable S-Stem: FAS divine law, destiny; FAS EST = it is right, necessary.

Fourth Declension

ARTUS, ARTUS (m) limb, joint.
CONSULATUS, CONSULATUS (m) the consulship, office of consul.
SENSUS, SENSUS (m) sense, ie one of the physical senses.
SONITUS, SONITUS (m) sound, noise.

Fifth Declension: DIES, DIEI (mf) day.

ADJECTIVES
First-Second Declension

ADVERSUS opposite, facing; perfect participle of ADVERTO (turn towards).
BEATUS blessed, fortunate; perfect participle of BEO (bless); comp BEATIOR, BEATIUS.
DEFESSUS exhausted; perfect participle of DEFATISCOR (become weary).
DELICATUS delicate, dainty; comp DELICATIOR, DELICATIUS.
DIVUS divine, deified.
GEMINUS twin, double.
HESTERNUS of yesterday; HESTERNUS DIES = yesterday.
INDOMITUS untamed, wild.
JUCUNDUS pleasant, jocund.
MEUS my, mine.
MOLESTUS annoying, troublesome.
MULTUS much, many; adv MULTUM.
MUTUUS mutual.
OTIOSUS full of OTIUM (leisure); at leisure, unoccupied.
SEMIMORTUUS half dead; from the perfect participle of MORIOR (die).
TUUS your, yours.

RUS > (E)R

MISER, MISERA, MISERUM miserable, wretched.
NOSTER, NOSTRA, NOSTRUM our, ours.

Third Declension
I-Stems

CURULIS, CURULE curule; literally, related to a chariot (CURRUS); the epithet of the special chair (SELLA CURULIS) in which higher magistrates sat when conducting hearings etc.
DULCIS, DULCE sweet; adv DULCE or DULCITER.
OMNIS, OMNE all, every.

TENUIS, TENUE thin, slight, fine.

One Termination

AUDAX (AUDACIS) bold, daring.
PAR (PARIS) equal.
VEMENS (VEMENTIS) vehement, violent; alt VEHEMENS.

Irregular comparative: PRIOR, PRIUS prior, previous; adv PRIUS
"previously", "in the past."

VERBS
First Conjugation

DEMANO, DEMANARE flow down (DEMANAT).
EXSULTO, EXSULTARE leap around, rejoice, go crazy (EXSULTAS).
IUVO, IUVARE help (IUVARET).
MOROR, MORARI, MORATUS delay, linger, wait (MORARIS).
ORO, ORARE beg, pray (ORAMUS).
PEJERO, PEJERARE swear falsely, commit perjury; alt PERJERO
(PEJERAT).
SPECTO, SPECTARE look at, gaze at (SPECTAT).
SUPERO, SUPERARE excel, be above.
TINTINO, TINTINARE ring (TINTINANT).
VERSO, VERSARE twist, turn over and over; frequentative of VERTO
(VERSARER).

Second Conjugation

CAVEO, CAVERE, CAVI beware of, be careful not to do something
(CAVE, CAVETO).
JACEO, JACERE, JACUI lie, recline (JACEBANT).
RIDEO, RIDERE, RISI laugh (RIDENTEM).
SEDEO, SEDERE, SEDI sit (SEDENS, SEDET).
TORPEO, TORPERE be sluggish, inactive (TORPET).
VIDEO, VIDERE, VIDI, VISUM see; passive, seem (VIDETUR).

Third Conjugation

DESPUO, DESPUERE spit back, reject (DESPUAS).
INCENDO, INCENDERE, INCENSI, INCENSUM set on fire, inflame.
IRASCOR, IRASCI, IRATUS become angry (IRASCERE).
LAEDO, LAEDERE, LAESI, LAESUM wound, injure.
LOQUOR, LOQUI, LOCUTUS say, speak, tell (LOQUERER).
LUDO, LUDERE, LUSI, LUSUM play, mock (LUSIMUS, LUDEBAT).
PERDO, PERDERE, PERDIDI, PERDITUM destroy, ruin (PERDIDIT).
REDDO, REDDERE, REDDIDI, REDDITUM give back, return (REDDENS).
REPOSCO, REPOSCERE demand back, ask in return (REPOSCAT).
SCRIBO, SCRIBERE, SCRIPSI, SCRIPTUM write (SCRIBENS).
TEGO, TEGERE, TEXI, TECTUM cover (TEGUNTUR, TEGERET).

NOUNS
First Declension
Feminine

CORONA crown; a circle of spectators around a speaker's platform.
FEMELLA girl; diminutive of FEMINA.
LINGUA tongue.
LOQUELLA speech.
PAPILLA nipple, breast.
PUELLA girl.
TENEBRAE shadows, darkness; plural forms only.

SECOND DECLENSION
Masculine

AMICUS friend.
CAMPUS field; the campus in Rome was the Campus Martius, the exercise field outside the city walls on the banks of the Tiber.
CIRCUS ring, circle; racetrack; the Circus in Rome was the Circus Maximus.
DEUS god (nom pl DI; gen DEORUM or DEUM; dat/abl DIIS or DIS).
ERUS master; reading retained by M at 54.2.
IAMBUS iamb, a poetic foot.
LIBELLUS booklet, diminutive of LIBER.

Persons

CALVUS Gaius Licinius Calvus, Catullus' friend, famous for his prosecution of Vatinius; see segment 6 and Vatinius in segment 19.
CAMERIUS Catullus' elusive friend in poems 55 and 58B.
FUFIDIUS an elderly supporter of Caesar; alt FUFICIUS.
HIRRUS Q's conjecture at 54.2; possibly C. Lucilius Hirrus, a cousin of Pompey.

NEUTER

PALATUM palate, mouth.
PEDITUM crepitus ventris, fart; perfect participle of PEDO (break wind).
SALAPUTIUM little man, midget.
TEMPLUM temple.

Third Declension
Nasal Stems (N)

AMBULATIO, AMBULATIONIS (f) walking around; place to walk.
CRIMEN, CRIMINIS (n) charge, crime.

Persons: LIBO, LIBONIS (m) and OTHO, OTHONIS (m) supporters of Caesar.

Liquid Stems (L,R)

AMOR, AMORIS (m) love.
IMPERATOR, IMPERATORIS (m) commander, general.
JUPPITER (m) the form of Jupiter's name used in exclamations and as the nominative case; other cases formed on Jov-: genitive, JOVIS; dative, JOVI etc.
LABOR, LABORIS (m) work, labor; archaic nominative LABOS.

S-Stems

CRUS, CRURIS (n) shin; leg.
OS, ORIS (n) mouth, face.
VENUS, VENERIS (f) Venus, the goddess of love.

Dental Stems (D, T)

CAPUT, CAPITIS (n) head.
FORS, FORTIS (f) chance, luck; adv FORTE by chance.

I-Stems

HERCULES, HERCULIS Hercules, the legendary hero; old gen HERCULI.
SENEX, SENIS (m) an old man.

Palatal Stem (C, G): LUX, LUCIS (f) light.

Fourth Declension

FASTUS, FASTUS (m) pride, arrogance.
FRUCTUS, FRUCTUS (m) fruit, benefit.
MANUS, MANUS (f) hand.
VULTUS, VULTUS (m) face.

ADJECTIVES
First-Second Declension

DISERTUS eloquent.
LACTEOLUS little milky; diminutive of LACTEUS from LAC (milk).
MAGNUS great; the cognomen of Pompey "the Great".
MEUS my, mine.
MIRIFICUS wonderful, marvellous; adv MIRIFICE.
MOLESTUS annoying, irritating.
NUDUS naked, nude.
PESSIMUS worst; superlative of MALUS.
PUSILLUS very small.
ROSEUS rosy.

RUSTICUS rustic.
SEMILAUTUS half washed, dirty; perfect participle of LAVO (wash).
SERENUS serene, peaceful.
SUMMUS highest.
TUUS your, yours.
UNICUS unique, only.
VATINIANUS Vatinian, of or like Vatinius; see segment 19.
VERBOSUS verbose, talkative.
VERUS true; M's reading at 55.22.

RUS > (E)R: VESTER, VESTRA, VESTRUM your, yours.

Third Declension
I-Stems

LEVIS, LEVE light.
OMNIS, OMNE all, every.
SUBTILIS, SUBTILE subtle, fine.

One Termination

AUDAX (AUDACIS) bold, daring; adv AUDACTER.
INMERENS (INMERENTIS) not deserving; alt IMMERENS.
PARTICEPS (PARTICIPIS) sharing in (+ genitive), participating.

Irregular comparative: MINOR, MINUS (gen MINORIS) smaller, less; comp of PARVUS.

VERBS
First Conjugation

ADMIROR, ADMIRARI, ADMIRATUS admire, wonder at (ADMIRANS).
DEMONSTRO, DEMONSTRARE point out, show (DEMONSTRES).
EXPLICO, EXPLICARE explain (EXPLICAVISSET > EXPLICASSET).
FLAGITO, FLAGITARE demand (FLAGITABAM).
NEGO, NEGARE deny (NEGAS).
OBSERO, OBSERARE close, bolt, lock (OBSERES).
ORO, ORARE beg, pray (ORAMUS).
SACRO, SACRARE consecrate, make holy (SACRATO).

Second Conjugation

DISPLICEO, DISPLICERE displease, be displeasing to (with dative).
GAUDEO, GAUDERE, GAVISUS rejoice, be pleased (GAUDET).
LATEO, LATERE, LATUI lie hidden (LATET).
LICET, LICERE, LICUIT impersonal, it is permissible (+ infin).
RIDEO, RIDERE, RISI laugh.
TENEO, TENERE, TENUI, TENTUM hold, keep (TENENT, TENES).
VIDEO, VIDERE, VIDI, VISUM see.

Third Conjugation

CLAUDO, CLAUDERE, CLAUSI, CLAUSUM close (CLAUSO).
COMMITTO, COMMITTERE, COMMISI, COMMISSUM commit, entrust; commit an action (COMMITTE).
CREDO, CREDERE, CREDIDI, CREDITUM believe (CREDE).
DICO, DICERE, DIXI, DICTUM, say, speak, tell (DIC).
EDO, EDERE, EDIDI, EDITUM give forth, put out, emit (EDE).
FERO, FERRE, TULI, LATUM carry, bear.
IRASCOR, IRASCI, IRATUS be angry (IRASCERE).
PRENDO, PRENDERE, PRENDI, PRENSUM seize, snatch, catch.
QUAERO, QUAERERE, QUAESIVI, QUAESITUM seek.
RECOQUO, RECOQUERE, RECOXI, RECOCTUM cook or boil again; RECOCTUS an adjective of uncertain pejorative sense -- "reheated."
REDUCO, REDUCERE, REDUXI, REDUCTUM lead back, draw back (REDUC...)
TOLLO, TOLLERE, SUSTULI, SUBLATUM lift up, remove (TOLLENS).

Third Conjugation IO: PROICIO, PROICERE, PROJECI, PROJECTUM cast forth, throw out (PROICIES).

Fourth Conjugation: NESCIO, NESCIRE not know, be ignorant; NESCIO QUIS (I know not who) = someone.

Irregular Verbs

AIO say, assert (AIT).
INQUAM irregular verb, say; used for direct quotations (INQUIT).
SUM, ESSE, FUI, FUTURUS be (EST, SINT, SIM, SIS FUTURUS).
VOLO, VELLE, VOLUI wish, be willing, desire (VIS, VELLEM).

NOUNS
First Declension
Feminine

ANGIPORTA narrow street, alley.
BIGAE team of horses; chariot team; plural forms only.
CENA dinner.
LEAENA lioness.
MACULA spot, stain.
MEDULLA marrow of a bone or the innermost part of anything.
PUELLA girl.
PUELLULA little girl; diminutive of PUELLA.

Persons

DIONA Dione, Venus' mother.
LESBIA Catullus' mistress.
RUFA a woman from Bologna.
SCYLLA a legendary monster occupying the straits between Italy
and Sicily; a nymph from the waist up, her lower body consisted
of six dog heads and pairs of paws with which she devoured
passing sailors.

Masculine

LADAS a legendarily fast runner in Alexander's army; Greek first
declension masculine: LADAS, LADAE, etc.
MAMURRA a Roman knight who grew wealthy in Caesar's service; see
segment 11.

SECOND DECLENSION
Masculine

AMICUS friend.
CACHINNUS laughter, a laugh.
LECTICULUS = LECTULUS little bed, couch; diminutive of LECTUS.
PUPULUS little boy.
ROGUS funeral pyre.
SOCIUS ally.
VENTUS wind.

Persons

CAELIUS possibly Marcus Caelius Rufus, a young man who is known
from Cicero's Pro Caelio to have had a love affair with Clodia
Pulchra, "Lesbia".
CAMERIUS Catullus' elusive friend in poems 55 and 58B.
CATULLUS the author.
MENENUS Rufa's husband.

PERSEUS Perseus, the legendary founder of Myceneae and slayer of
Medusa; Mercury loaned him winged sandals.
REMUS Romulus' brother.
RHESUS a king of Thrace mentioned in the Iliad, famed for his
chariot and horses, which are stolen by Diomedes and Odysseus in
book 10.
RUFULUS diminutive of RUFUS the cognomen "red" of an unknown man,
possibly Caelius.

RUS > (E)R: ADULTER, ADULTERI adulterer.

NEUTER

QUADRIVIUM crossroads, intersection.
SEPULCRETUM graveyard, cemetery.
TELUM javelin, pike.

Third Declension

Dental Stems (D,T)

COR, CORDIS (n) heart.
CUSTOS, CUSTODIS (mf) guard.
MENS, MENTIS (f) mind.
MONS, MONTIS (m) mountain.
NEPOS, NEPOTIS (mf) grandchild, descendant.
PARS, PARTIS (f) part.

Liquid Stems (L,R)

LANGUOR, LANGUORIS (m) weakness, faintness; alt LANGOR.
USTOR, USTORIS (m) burner; a servant who attended to funeral
pyres, cemetery attendant.
UXOR, UXORIS (f) wife.

Person: CAESAR, CAESARIS Gaius Julius Caesar, the later dictator.

I-Stems

AURIS, AURIS (f) ear.
IGNIS, IGNIS (m) fire.
PANIS, PANIS (m) bread.
RIVALIS, RIVALIS (m) rival.

Nasal Stems

INGUEN, INGUINIS (n) groin, genitals.

Person: CATO, CATONIS probably Valerius Cato, a grammarian and
poet, commemorated by Furius Bibaculus as the "Latin Siren," a
person who both taught poets and wrote poetry. Furius also

ridiculed him for his poverty; see Furius in segment 10.

Palatal Stem (C, G): VOX, VOCIS (f) voice.

Fourth Declension

CASUS, CASUS (m) fall, that which befalls, circumstance, chance.
CURSUS, CURSUS (m) running, motion; course.
VOLATUS, VOLATUS (m) flight.

Fifth Declension: RES, REI (f) thing, affair, situation.

ADJECTIVES
First-Second Declension

CINAEDUS loose, wanton, amoral.
CITUS rapid, fast; perfect participle of CIEO (arouse).
DEFESSUS exhausted; perfect participle of DEFATISCOR (become weary).
DIGNUS worthy, worthy of (with ablative).
DURUS hard.
ERUDITULUS rather skillful, somewhat proficient; diminutive of ERUDITUS (erudite, learned).
FORMIANUS of or from FORMIAE, a town in the vicinity of Rome.
FERUS wild, fierce.
GEMELLUS little twin, diminutive of GEMINUS.
IMPROBUS improper, immoral.
INFIMUS lowest; superlative of INFERUS.
JOCOSUS full of jokes, funny, enjoyable.
LIBYSTINUS Libyan.
MAGNANIMUS magnanimous, noble.
MIRUS marvellous, admirable, wonderful.
MORBOSUS full of disease, sick; from MORBUS (disease).
MULTUS much, many.
NIVEUS snowy, snow-white.
NOVUS new, strange; superlative NOVISSIMUS latest, most recent.
PATHICUS pathic, passively homosexual.
PEGASEUS Pegasean, of or like Pegasus, the flying horse of mythology.
RIDICULUS ridiculous, laughable.
RIGIDUS rigid, stiff.
SEMIRASUS half shaved, seedy; from the perfect participle of RADO (scrape, shave).
SUUS his, her, its or their own.
TUUS your, yours.
URBANUS urbane; of or from the city.

RUS > (E)R

NOSTER, NOSTRA, NOSTRUM our, ours.
PULCHER, PULCHRA, PULCHRUM beautiful; adv PULCRE or PULCHRE.

TAETER, TAETRA, TAETRUM foul, disgusting, gross.

Third Declension
I-Stems

BONONIENSIS, BONONIENSE of or from Bononia, modern Bologna.
OMNIS, OMNE all, every.
VOLATILIS, VOLATILE flying.

One Termination

CRES (CRETIS) Cretan.
PAR (PARIS) equal; adv PARITER.
PINNIPES (PINNIPEDIS) having winged feet.
PLUMIPES (PLUMIPEDIS) having plumed or feathered feet.
PLUS more; in the singular only the neuter accusative/adverbial
form PLUS occurs; plural forms: PLURES, PLURA etc.
SUPPLEX (SUPPLICIS) suppliant, humble.
VORAX (VORACIS) voracious, greedy; comp VORACIOR, VORACIUS.

VERBS
First Conjugation

AMO, AMARE love (AMAS, AMAVIT).
DICO, DICARE dedicate to, present (DICARES).
ELEVO, ELEVARE lighten, remove; excuse (ELEVENTUR).
FELLO, FELLARE suck (FELLAT).
LATRO, LATRARE bark (LATRANS).
PROCREO, PROCREARE give birth to, bring forth (PROCREAVIT).
QUAERITO, QUAERITARE search for; frequentative of QUAERO
(QUAERITANDO).
TRUSO, TRUSARE push at repeatedly; frequentative of TRUDO
(TRUSANTEM).

Second Conjugation

HABEO, HABERE, HABUI, HABITUM have (HABERES).
PLACEO, PLACERE, PLACUI please (PLACET).
RESIDEO, RESIDERE, RESEDI sit back, settle down, remain
(RESIDENT).
RIDEO, RIDERE, RISI laugh (RIDE).
VIDEO, VIDERE, VIDI, VISUM see (VIDISTIS).

Third Conjugation

ADDO, ADDERE, ADDIDI, ADDITUM add (ADDE)
CAEDO, CAEDERE, CECIDI, CAESUM cut, cut down, kill.
CONTEMNO, CONTEMNERE, CONTEMPSI, CONTEMPTUM despise, contemn
(CONTEMPTAM).
DEPRENDO, DEPRENDERE, DEPRENDI, DEPRENSUM seize, catch hold of.
DEVOLVO, DEVOLVERE, DEVOLVI, DEVOLUTUM roll down or away.

ELUO, ELUERE, ELUTUM wash away (ELUENTUR).
FERO, FERRE, TULI, LATUM carry, bear (FERAR).
FINGO, FINGERE, FINXI, FICTUM shape, mould, form (FINGAR).
GLUBO, GLUBERE peel, skin (GLUBIT).
IMPRIMO, IMPRIMERE, IMPRESSI, IMPRESSUM press in or upon
(IMPRESSAE).
JUNGO, JUNGERE, JUNXI, JUNCTUM join, yoke, harness (JUNCTOS).
PEREDO, PERESSE, PEREDI, PERESUM eat away, consume.
PROSEQUOR, PROSEQUI, PROSECUTUS follow after, chase (PROSEQUENS).
REQUIRO, REQUIRERE, REQUISII, REQUISITUM seek, look for
(REQUIRE).
TUNDO, TUNDERE, TUTUDI, TUSUM strike, beat (TUNDERETUR).

Third Conjugation IO: RAPIO, RAPERE, RAPUI, RAPTUM seize, take,
steal.

Fourth Conjugation

CONVENIO, CONVENIRE, CONVENI come together; impersonal CONVENIT
it suits, it is agreed or agreeable.
VINCIO, VINCIRE, VINXI, VINCTUM bind, tie (VINCTOS).

Irregular Verb: SUM, ESSE, FUI (ESSEM, EST).